What Works:
A New Approach to Program and Policy Analysis

What Works:
A New Approach to Program and Policy Analysis

Kenneth J. Meier
Texas A&M University

Jeff Gill
University of Florida

Westview Press
A Member of the Perseus Books Group

All rights reserved. Printed in the United States of America. No part of this publication may
be reproduced or transmitted in any form or by any means, electronic or mechanical, including
photocopy, recording, or any information storage and retrieval system, without permission
in writing from the publisher.

Copyright© 2000 by Westview Press, a member of the Perseus Books Group.

Published in 2000 in the United States of America by Westview Press,
5500 Central Avenue, Boulder, Colorado 80301-2877,
and in the United Kingdom by Westview Press,
12 Hid's Copse Road, Cumnor Hill, Oxford OX2 9JJ

A Catalog-in-Publication record for this title is available from the Library of Congress.
ISBN 0-8133-9781-2.

The paper used in this publication meets the requirements of the American National Standards for
Permanence of Paper for Printed Library Materials Z39.48-1984.

10   9   8   7   6   5   4   3   2   1

Ken Meier dedicates this book to Laura Langbein.
Jeff Gill dedicates this book to James A. Thurber.

Contents

Preface   xi

1   ZEN AND THE ART OF POLICY ANALYSIS: SUBSTANTIVELY WEIGHTED ANALYTICAL TECHNIQUES   1

1.1   Introduction   1

1.2   Sciences of the Artificial   2

1.3   A Graphical Overview   3

1.4   Heterogeneity Is Good   5

1.5   The Zen of Weighting   7

1.6   Why Not Just Run Separate Regressions?   8

1.7   Don't Throw Away Your Other Tools   10

1.8   When Not to Use SWAT   10

     1.8.1   Case 1: No Residual Variation   11

     1.8.2   Case 2: When There Is a Clear Break Between Two Sets of Programs   11

     1.8.3   Case 3: An Incorrect Functional Form   12

1.9   Plan of the Book   13

1.10   Discussion   14

1.11   References   14

2   AN INTRODUCTION TO SUBSTANTIVELY WEIGHTED LEAST SQUARES   17

2.1   Introduction   17

2.2   Child Support Enforcement   18

2.3   The Original Study   19

2.4   Regression Diagnostics   21

2.5   Robust and Resistant Regression   24

2.6   SWLS   27

viii   *Contents*

2.7   Some Caveats   34

2.8   SWAT Versus Best Practices   34

2.9   SWAT Versus L-Regression: A Methodological Interlude   35

2.10 But So What?   36

2.11 Addendum: Data Description   37

2.12 References   38

3   THE THEORY AND APPLICATION OF GENERALIZED SUBSTANTIVELY REWEIGHTED LEAST SQUARES   41

3.1   Introduction   41

3.2   Distribution of the Jackknifed Residuals   43

3.3   Relationship to the F Distribution   45

3.4   Five Assumptions and a Warning   47

3.5   Using the GSRLS Procedure   48

3.6   A Simple Example   50

3.7   SWAT Versus the Chow Test   55

3.8   Discussion   56

3.9   Addendum: Splus/R Code for SWAT   57

3.10 References   58

4   SUBSTANTIVELY WEIGHTED ANALYTICAL TECHNIQUES FOR SUCCESSES AND FAILURES: SWLS AND GSRLS   59

4.1   Introduction   59

4.2   The Dataset   61

    4.2.1   The Outcome Variable   61

    4.2.2   The Explanatory Variables   61

4.3   SWLS Findings   64

4.4   GSRLS Results   71

4.5   Differences Between SWLS and GSRLS   71

4.6   Discussion   78

4.7   References   78

Contents   ix

5 SEPARATING EXCELLENT AGENCIES FROM THE GOOD ONES: PUSHING THE EXTREMES OF THE DATA DISTRIBUTION   83

5.1 Introduction   83

5.2 An Education Production Function   85

5.3 Linear Model Findings   85

5.4 The Pretty Good Agencies   86

5.5 The Super Agencies   89

5.6 Lucky or Good?   90

5.7 What the Super Agencies Do Differently   92

5.8 Extensions   96

5.9 Discussion   97

5.10 References   97

6 WEIGHTING WITH AN EXOGENOUS VARIABLE OR WITH TWO EXOGENOUS VARIABLES: EQUITY VERSUS EXCELLENCE IN ORGANIZATIONS   99

6.1 Introduction   99

6.2 The Theoretical Setting for the Study   100

6.3 Educational Performance   101

    6.3.1 The Outcome Variable   102

    6.3.2 Explanatory Variables   103

6.4 Substantively Weighted Least Squares   104

6.5 Findings   104

6.6 Weighting in Two Dimensions   112

6.7 Two-Dimensional Weights: An Illustration   113

6.8 Discussion   115

6.9 References   116

7 SWAT IN POOLED ANALYSIS   119

7.1 Introduction   119

7.2 Zen and the Art of Pooling   120

7.3 The Full—and Then Some—Prison Blues   123

7.4 Looking at the Data   125

7.5 Applying SWAT to the Data   127

    7.5.1 A Note of Caution   130

x   Contents

     7.5.2   The Winners: The Low Crime States   131

     7.5.3   The Losers: High Crime States   134

7.6   Path Dependence   138

7.7   A Second Example: Educational Performance   138

7.8   Discussion   143

7.9   Addendum: Data Description   143

7.10 References   145

8   THE ZEN AND THE PRACTICE: SOME FINAL REMARKS   147

8.1   Overview   147

8.2   The Secret Life of Residuals   148

8.3   Weighting the Artificial   149

8.4   Hypotheses   150

8.5   If I Had a Hammer   151

8.6   The Final Word   152

8.7   References   153

Index   155

Preface

This book is intended to introduce a new methodological approach, substantively weighted analytical techniques (SWAT), to analyzing data. This approach is focused on investigating subgroups in a given sample with the idea that what makes them different can be important. The differences are often of key substantive importance, such as which programs or agencies are performing at an unexpectedly high level given their available resources. This investigation of "what works" is typically interesting to both researchers and practitioners in public administration. Consequently we have written this book in such a way as to appeal to both audiences. This orientation relies heavily on real and practical examples as a way of illustrating SWAT techniques.

The SWAT philosophy is new to data analysis and will be uncomfortable to some readers. Underpinning this way of thinking is the idea of a "hypothetical population" of interest rather than the actual, existing population from which the data are drawn. We posit the idea that investigating typical cases is not only uninteresting in some settings, but also provides little prescriptive advice.

Many of the methods used in the analysis of policy or programs are inappropriate, and some are actually misleading. The methods used in public administration and public policy should be determined by the needs of the analyst and the desire to make policy recommendations, not by tradition in writing econometric textbooks. We think a great deal of progress can be made by consciously thinking about what we want quantitative methods to tell us and then seeking out or inventing methods that do exactly that. One of the major problems with contemporary policy analysis is the overemphasis on average cases. Although the average case contains a great deal of useful policy information, it is often not the case or set of cases that concern us the most. More often, we care about exceptional cases—agencies that perform well, programs that are likely to collapse, or programs that can meet more than one goal simultaneously, for example. SWAT was invented to look at such cases and to tease out how they differ from the average case. We think there is a great deal of policy-relevant information in such cases. Whenever one of us demonstrates SWAT methods to an individual, we get one of two predictable reactions. First, many people respond positively, noting that, "Yes, SWAT is telling me something I would like to know." A second group of people take refuge in the language of statistics and make statements such as "Those have to be biased estimators" or

xi

xii   Preface

"I'll bet heteroscedasticity is a major problem." The second response troubles us because it immediately assumes that our goal is estimation and inference in the classical manner of statistics (despite our frequent and emphasized statements that SWAT does neither) and because it represents what we see as a rigid and uncreative approach to methods.

Complex public problems require creative and flexible analysis. The rigid application of techniques that make heroic assumptions presents one picture of public programs, but it is only one picture, and perhaps not even an interesting picture. SWAT is not only a technique but also a philosophy of analysis. It seeks to guide analysts in looking at their data in different ways to see what those looks reveal that is new and interesting. This book presents SWAT in the context of exploratory data analysis. We view it as a qualitative tool that uses quantitative data. The exploratory data analysis approach is only one of four ways that SWAT can be viewed. It can also be viewed as an estimation technique for hypothetical populations, as a merger of sensitivity analysis with traditional techniques, or as a cross-sectional version of time-varying-parameter techniques. A brief discussion of these other ways to motivate SWAT is merited to illustrate the logic of the technique.

Classical inference asks: given a population P, what is the probability that sample S was drawn from it? SWAT reweights outlier cases (or any cases of special interest) so that SWAT results cannot say anything about whether or not S could be drawn from P. The coefficients in SWAT quite clearly cannot be inferential estimates of any population parameters in P. However, one might envision a different population, say, P*, that contains ten times the number of high-performing cases and only one-tenth the number of non-high-performing cases. SWAT, by reweighting cases accordingly, might well provide parameter estimates for P*, but P* is a hypothetical population, not one that currently exists. That hypothetical population has an assumed composition based on the SWAT weights assigned and the results will strongly reflect those assumptions.

The second alternative way to think about SWAT is simply that it is a constrained form of sensitivity analysis. Statistics are estimates with an associated variance. Any specific point estimate has an associated standard error. The sensitivity of the point estimate to changes in the composition of the data tells the researcher a great deal about the robustness of a relationship. Influence and leverage diagnostics are constructed via this logic. SWAT coefficients can be viewed in the same light. By altering the composition of the sample, especially with the iterative weighting process, one can judge how stable or unstable coefficients are. Although stability is usually highly valued when sensitivity analysis is done, in SWAT we seek the instability because that is also informative.

A third possible way to think about SWAT is the flexible generalized least squares approach to time-varying parameters. That approach suggests that not only do relationships between variables vary over time, but also that the relationship might actually be unique for each time period. SWAT in essence takes this idea and applies it to cross-sectional patterns. Relationships in the SWAT context are expected to vary across different types of organizations. The cluster of the different relationships and how they diverge from the average relationship is useful information to the analyst. Our emphasis on flexible approaches to analysis is illustrated throughout the book as we change weighting schemes, look at data in different ways, change the types of values we wish to emphasize, and compare various ways of accomplishing similar methodological tasks. Flexibility in our mind avoids bad habits. Analysis should be constantly adapted to the substantive needs of the problem. The reader will quickly note that we avoid significance testing in this text. In part, this reflects our interest in flexible approaches to analysis; traditional hypothesis testing is generally done by rote with little thought about what is actually being tested. But more important, we believe that hypothesis testing as it is done in the social sciences is both misguiding and misleading.

Throughout this book we avoid the use of p-values and their even more flawed cousin, "stars." The severely flawed practice of "null hypothesis significance testing" in the social sciences has greatly hindered the research process for over 40 years (Gill 1999), and we see no reason to perpetuate the practice here. Instead, we rely on the theoretically and practically superior approach of reporting parameter uncertainty through confidence intervals. The reader determined to view results in terms of p-values can rely upon the principle that a 95% confidence interval that is bounded away from zero (i.e., does not contain the origin) is functionally equivalent to a p-value less than 0.05.

Chapter 1 introduces the "Zen" of SWAT analysis. This is the most fundamental and therefore important chapter in this book. Rereading Chapter 1 is seldom a waste of time as the message contained therein is key to understanding this new perspective. Chapter 2 introduces the first example, and details the most basic SWAT technique: substantively weighted least squares. This chapter demonstrates that SWAT is useful in practical settings by identifying key organizational factors that lead to program success. Chapter 3 presents the formal mathematical and statistical background for SWAT. Although SWAT is essentially a *qualitative* approach, it is based on basic quantitative theory. This chapter can be skipped on the first reading with little loss of continuity. We do, however, recommend that these principles be understood by regular users of the method. Chapter 4 provides a nuanced example using educational testing data. The primary message is that different subgroups can be identified and studied in the SWAT context. Chapter 5 varies the basic SWAT method to sort out not just high-performing cases, but also extremely high-performing cases. This application is interesting because there are often important differences in how "superstar" organizations behave. Chapter 6 introduces the idea that multiple criteria for segmentation can be used in SWAT. This means that the SWAT-oriented data analyst has great flexibility in how categories of interest are defined. Chapter 7 further illustrates the flexibility

xiv   *Preface*

of SWAT by applying the method to pooled and time series data, showing that traditional variations on data analysis are easily incorporated. In Chapter 8 we wrap up with some admonitions and concluding remarks.

A large number of persons provided assistance to us in a variety of ways in this project. We have exploited our coauthors a great deal in the process of applying SWAT techniques to various problems. To recognize the efforts of Lael Keiser, George Waller, J. L. "Bubba" Polinard, Robert D. Wrinkle, and Kevin Smith, we have listed them as coauthors on chapters that grew out of their work. A large number of individuals either commented on individual chapters or SWAT in general, including Gary King, Bert Kritzer, Larry Bartels, Jonathan Nagler, Neal Beck, Michael Licari, and seminar participants at the University of New Mexico, the University of Missouri, and the University of Texas at Dallas. Nick Theobald and John Bohte provided research assistance. We thank Stu Bretschneider for calling to our attention the contrast between SWAT and L-regression. These comments have improved our thinking about SWAT and methods in general. We also thank Leo Wiegman and the rest of the people at Westview Press for their support and assistance. As is now tradition in the social sciences, Paul Sabatier has agreed to take responsibility for all remaining errors in this book.

Ken Meier

College Station, TX

Jeff Gill

Gainesville, FL

Chapter 1

Zen and the Art of Policy Analysis: Substantively Weighted Analytical Techniques

Kenneth J. Meier, Jeff Gill

1.1 Introduction

The supposition that public managers seek to identify and emulate the average performing case is simply wrong. Yet the same public manager will diligently analyze quantitative data related to the performance of his or her agency with tools that focus on the behavior of *typical and undistinguished cases*. In this book we seek to liberate managers and policy analysts from the burden of a dominant methodology developed in the social sciences over fifty years ago and long abandoned by sophisticated research methodologists. Our solution, Substantively Weighted Analytical Techniques (SWAT), takes a counterintuitive and untraditional approach to the treatment of atypical cases in the data. It seeks to take the typical results of linear analysis and apply systematic *qualitative* techniques in a creative manner.

Substantively Weighted Analytical Techniques are a related set of statistical procedures that seek to generate information more useful to policy analysts.[1] The techniques generally involve weighting data to reveal how certain organizations, programs, or policies differ in their impact on their target populations. It may be thought of as a form of regression diagnostics with a different twist. Rather than avoiding the unusual and seeking the safety of techniques that are highly resistant to outlying cases, SWAT encourages the analyst to seek out the unusual cases and understand the valuable information that they contain.

Because SWAT techniques conceptualize such notions as bias, estimation, and statistical analysis in ways different from the classical approach to statistics, we believe that the approach requires what is essentially a different way of thinking about quantitative methods and their role in the social sciences. This chapter describes the Zen, the philosophy that underlies SWAT as a set of analytical techniques. While such a chapter is unusual in a methodological text, it really should not be. All statistical analyses combine technical competence with the art of practice. Anyone can take data, look up the (hopefully) appropriate formulae, and calculate results. As statistical software packages become increasingly easy to use, analysts tend to rely on computational tools to the detriment of human model specification and interpretation. The value of statistical results, however, depends on the art of the analyst, how well the analyst has perceived the problem, how well the study fits the data-generating process, and how much creativity the analyst brings to the problem. Even though mechanical techniques are far easier to teach than the Zen of analysis, without an understanding of the philosophy of analysis, no technique will produce more than the sound of one hand clapping.

We liken our enterprise to playing with the data just as a jazz soloist manipulates a melody to stretch its limits and seek its potential. To more classically trained analysts, we may appear to be playing our instruments out of tune. Our response is "patience." Judge our approach by whether or not it provides useful information about programs and policies. When Bob Wills added drums to western swing, it also violated accepted traditions; but it eventually spawned an entire genre of music. The proof of SWAT is in the performance: does it tell one something new that was not obvious before?

1.2 Sciences of the Artificial

Herbert Simon (1969) argued that social sciences are sciences of the artificial; that is, they are design sciences, concerned not just with what is, but also with what

---

[1]We are using the term *policy analyst* to cover any individual who is interested in both the scientific study of a phenomenon and how that phenomenon might be changed. This definition covers parts or all of several social sciences, some physical sciences, and most professions. The term is used here as a matter of convenience.

might be. Such a statement is controversial; every social science contains individuals who strongly advocate emulation of the physical sciences with their perceived focus on theory testing and analysis to provide purely theoretical knowledge. At the same time, others seek knowledge so that they can redesign programs, fix policy problems, or offer advice to the relevant powers that be. Despite these differences, policy analysts with practical and immediate prescriptive needs are still using tools indistinguishable from those favored by researchers with theoretical and abstract concerns.

While the general perception is that theoretically focused researchers are more advanced methodologically than those who seek prescriptive leverage, we feel that the *reverse* should be true. Individuals with normative concerns, those who seek to give policy advice, need to be better methodologists than those interested solely in building empirical theory. The reason is simple. The policy analyst/prescriptive scientist must not only be able to explain regularities but must also be able to isolate factors that, when changed, produce the desired results. Identifying causal relationships is inherently a more difficult process than finding statistical regularities. In the policy sphere, people design and redesign programs to change the status quo. This suggests a concern with maximizing performance rather than minimizing variance.

The policy analyst needs to recognize that developments in statistical methodology have been driven by the more traditional needs of empirical scholars rather than by policy concerns. As a result, the development of more elaborate methods may or may not be of value to the policy analyst and may often benefit the policy analyst only by accident.

SWAT is an analytical approach unabashedly designed for the sciences of the artificial. It asks why has agency X performed better than other similar agencies. It asks what variables can be manipulated to produce better results. It asks whether some agencies/organizations do something different with their resources, something that could be transplanted to other organizations.

1.3 A Graphical Overview

Linear modeling techniques form the core of both policy analysis and the social sciences in general. This is because of their theoretical simplicity (Greene 1999) and adaptability (Fahrmeir and Tutz 1994; McCullagh and Nelder 1983). However, a significant amount of work in the more advanced methodological literature has sought to develop nonlinear analytic tools such as generalized additive models (Hastie and Tibshirani 1990), nonparametric density estimation (Scott 1992; Cleveland 1993), qualitative choice models (Amemiya 1985), spatial models (Anselin 1988), and a resurgence of Bayesian modeling due to inexpensive computing time (Gelman et al. 1995; Box and Tiao 1992; Gamerman 1997; Tanner 1996), just to name a few.

In essence, linear regression models estimate a mean impact on the outcome variable for a one-unit change in an explanatory variable—such as, for example, what impact does a specified change in a welfare-to-work program have on the average employment of former welfare recipients? To illustrate, in Panel 1, Figure 1.1, we have graphed the rate of organizational learning for child support agencies on the Y-axis and the inputs to the agency on the X-axis. Because organizational learning is measured by the increase in child support collections per capita per year, it is also a performance measure. This relationship of inputs to outputs forms the core of most policy analyses.

Although linear regression techniques are often sensitive to outlying cases (Rousseeuw and Leroy 1987; Andrews 1974), when the technique is done well with the correct diagnostics, it generates a great deal of information about a hypothetical average case, provided the data fit a linear pattern. The resulting statistical model well describes typical cases or typical behavior in the data. A classic example is shown in Panel 1, Figure 1.1, where the case closest to the average is marked with the letters "SD" indicating South Dakota. While this information is always valuable in terms of testing theories, there are prescriptive situations where such information may not be useful. For example, point MI (Michigan) already outperforms the average state by a substantial amount. Just

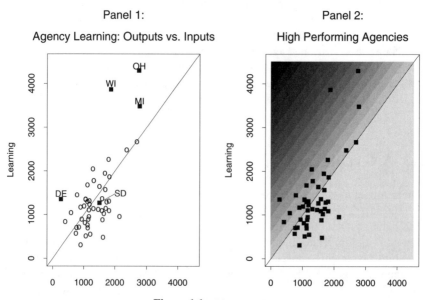

Figure 1.1 Linear Model

1 Zen and the Art of Policy Analysis: Substantively Weighted Analytical Techniques   5

as the U.S. Army does not seek to emulate the Iraqi Army, Michigan might be able to learn some things from South Dakota, but the odds are not favorable. Of more interest to Michigan is the agency for Ohio (OH), an agency that has the same relative level of inputs but a much higher output level. Even Wisconsin (WI) might have some value to Michigan since it produces a higher level output with far fewer resources.

SWAT seeks to change the approach to analysis from focusing exclusively on the average case to providing some focus on those cases that are above average (or below average in other situations). These cases include those in Panel 2 of Figure 1.1 that are within the gradually shaded region; each of these cases produces more learning than one would expect given the inputs they have. The more extreme the shading, the more atypical the enclosed case is for a linear model. This sense of continuously increasing specialty of cases is exactly what SWAT is designed to detect and analyze. All of these atypical points are above the regression line, which essentially summarizes the expected level of output for a given level of inputs. The key cases include not only high achievers such as Wisconsin and Ohio, but also cases like Delaware (DE) that perform reasonably well despite having a very low level of inputs.

The two panels in Figure 1.1 show, for the same data, alternate ways of high-lighting performance optimizers: agencies that perform better than expected. SWAT can be used to examine any subset of agencies or programs depending on the criterion of interest to the analyst. This text will illustrate its use with performance optimizers (Chapter 2), with failures and risk averse organizations (Chapter 4), with exceptional agencies rather than just good ones (Chapter 5), with organizations that perform yet do so equitably (Chapter 6), and with organizations that are stable and those that combine stability with high performance (Chapter 7). The appropriate subgroup to examine depends on the problem that needs to be addressed. SWAT is a context-dependent tool.

1.4 Heterogeneity Is Good

A standard linear regression analysis looks at the distances of individual points from a line and considers these as errors (also called disturbances or residuals). The method assumes that error values are independently normally distributed with mean zero and uncorrelated to explanatory variables in the model.[2] Conversely, SWAT considers these errors useful information that when properly examined can provide clues to program performance.

---

[2]Because regression also assumes no specification errors, this error should not be correlated with any variables that are not included in the model.

6   Kenneth J. Meier, Jeff Gill

Linear regression models assume that the relationship between two variables is the same for all cases. For example, suppose that a reduction in class size of one student per class is found to be associated with an additional 1 percent of students who pass competency exams. In regression this is an estimate of the average relationship; that is, all other things being equal, a reduction of one student in average class size is associated with an increase of 1 percent in students passing the exam.

SWAT approaches the regression errors in another manner. It assumes that the slope relating two variables actually varies for analyst-defined classes of programs. Using the same example, for a one-student reduction in class size, program A might have an increase in student pass rates of 1 percent; the corresponding figure for program B might be 0.7; for program C, 1.3; and for program D, 0.0 (see Table 1.1). Why might program C get 30 percent more improvement from a class size reduction than A? Many possibilities exist; program C might have better trained teachers, or more computer facilities, or an innovative curriculum, or a variety of other factors. The important element of this example is this: program A represents the average relationship, but C exceeds this performance. While turning all programs into the equivalent of A will benefit many of those served by the below average programs, it will do little for those programs that are more effective than A at translating reduction in class size into student performance.

Table 1.1   Slopes Varying by Programs

Program	A	B	C	D
Slope	1.0	0.7	1.3	0.0

These variations in relationships, therefore, are indicators of what might be possible by other programs. They are the what "might be" rather than the "what is." SWAT uses this assumption to examine how the slopes of programs that meet some criterion could differ from the slopes of other programs. It essentially uses weighting techniques to increase the influence of designated programs and to decrease the influence of the other programs in the analysis. This is done in a series of steps so that the analyst can observe how the slopes change and from that determine what the selected programs do different from what the other programs do.[3]

Looking at heterogeneity is often a good thing to do whether or not one is interested in prescription. Programs, agencies, and organizations are complex systems. One generally learns more about complex systems under extreme conditions than under normal conditions. Learning how organizations fail, for example, is difficult

---

[3]The specific procedures are discussed in subsequent chapters.

without pushing organizations to the point where many can and do fail. Similarly, learning what is potentially possible in a program can be done only by pushing the program to its limits. Many of the most interesting cases in policy analysis occur at the extremes.[4]

1.5 The Zen of Weighting

SWAT uses a criterion to weight cases of greater interest more heavily than cases of less interest. In some cases this criterion will be internal or endogenous to the model. In the first example, the criterion was high performance relative to the inputs the program received. We did not have an independent measure of high performance but rather inferred this criterion from the residuals of the regression. In this case, we use the regression itself to define the relevant cases and then will proceed to manipulate this regression to generate the SWAT results.

In other cases, the selection criterion will be a variable that is not included (inherently or directly) in the model. For example, in Chapter 6 we examine school districts that perform better than average subject to the constraint that they must be equitable (that is, that minority students should perform about as well as Anglo students). In cases such as this one where the criterion variable is exogenous to the model, then the SWAT procedure is simply to run weighted least squares regression using this exogenous variable to generate the changing weights.

The second element of weighting involves the size of the exemplary group. As an illustration, if one were interested in high-performance programs, one might select all programs above the regression line as the set of weighted programs. This would include about half of all programs, not an especially exclusive group. The proportion of programs included in the category of interest can be varied to fit the needs of the analyst. Some analysts will want to see how the top 20 percent or the top 10 percent or even the top 5 percent of the programs differ from the average programs. In Chapter 3 we relate this weighting criterion to the F-distribution so that an analyst can balance the proportion of cases in the select group against distributional assumptions. The size of the group selected must be determined by the substantive context being examined and the experience of managers and analysts.

Why, one might ask, would the analyst not always select a small, highly distinct group for weighting purposes? First, such decisions are also subject to limits of sample size. With small samples and a fairly high selection standard, one runs the risk of generalizing from too few cases. SWAT, unlike other techniques, can generate results with only a small number of cases. The analyst, not the statistical

---

[4]Policy analysis is a lot like life, and in the immortal words of Evel Knievel, "Life is not worth living without a lump in your throat and a knot in your stomach."

8   Kenneth J. Meier, Jeff Gill

program, decides how many cases to examine. Similar to all other methods, SWAT must be used in an informed manner. These programs might well be different for idiosyncratic reasons that cannot be transferred to other programs.

Second, one sometimes needs to address the Jack Nicklaus problem. When a young Jack Nicklaus was taking the professional golf tour by storm, legend Sam Snead was reputed to remark, "He plays a game with which I am not familiar." In other words, Nicklaus' skills and techniques were so different from those of Snead that Snead would have had difficulty in emulating them. Oftentimes improvements can be obtained incrementally when they cannot be obtained all at once. The below average program might be unable to learn from the exceptional program or even the above average program, but it may be able to emulate the average program. Once the transition to an average program has taken place, then perhaps the next step is possible.[5]

1.6 Why Not Just Run Separate Regressions?

If one feels that there are two (or more) types of programs, the often asked question is, why not run separate regressions on each set? Such a process essentially runs a linear regression on a subset of cases based on their residuals (or some other criterion), and is an analog to analyzing "alpha-trimmed" data.[6] A second approach, quantile regression is similar except it uses least absolute deviations rather than least squares as the base estimating technique. The quantile regression approach has a different philosophy about errors than does SWAT. It uses a resistant estimation technique and thus is not as sensitive to differences in performance at the extremes. To SWAT, the extremes are often the most interesting cases. We favor SWAT over these partitioned regression approaches for several reasons.

First, in many situations the number of cases is too small to divide into sub-samples and run partitioned regressions. If one has a model with seven variables and only fifty cases, then running a regression of the top 20 percent of cases is highly problematic. This is often a serious problem with the types of data sets encountered in public policy analysis. Conversely, political science and sociology data sets (American National Election Study, General Social Survey) often have thousands of cases and will not be affected by this limitation.

---

[5] We took this idea from Larry Mohr. In response to Professor Mohr's study on the impact of research grants on universities, he was asked what University of Michigan, an exceptional university in this regard, might learn from an average university. His subsequent counterargument about relative position and incremental change was quite convincing.

[6] For a discussion of this general problem and the justification for the iterative process rather than the separate regression process, see Bartels (1997). Quantile regression is discussed in Judge et al. (1985, p. 834). See also Miller (1984, 1990). Stu Bretschneider among others has called this question to our attention.

Second, the threshold or alpha-trim in partitioned regression is a completely subjective and arbitrary decision on the part of the analyst. Conversely, SWAT techniques allow the analyst to determine differing threshold levels, but in all cases link this decision to distribution theory, thereby remaining overt about the ramifications of determining levels.

Third, in some cases partitioned regression may produce results that are not meaningful. If the subset of cases is well distributed in terms of X values, then a situation such as that in Figure 1.2 is possible. In this case, rather than revealing that different programs have different slopes, partitioned regression would absorb the difference in the two sets of programs in the intercept. Such a result does not focus on specific variables that can be manipulated to generate better results. By retaining the average cases in the analysis, SWAT has an anchor in the linear regression results. This can be thought of as focusing on the desired cases but keeping them in the *context* of the entire data set. SWAT does not throw out data before they contribute to the model.

In some cases SWAT and partitioned regression produce similar results. The reason for this coincidence is essentially that partitioned regression can be considered a special case of SWAT where the average cases are weighted at 0 rather than at 0.05 or whatever ending criterion is specified by the analysis.

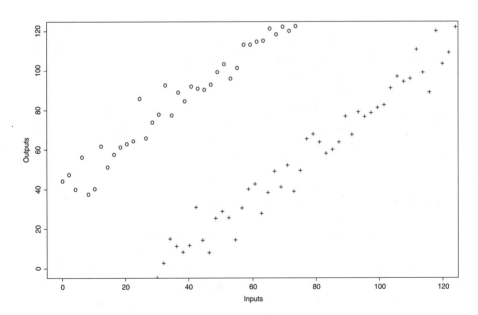

Figure 1.2 Parallel Relationships

Fourth, SWAT uses an iterative procedure, and this produces interesting information for the analyst. Chapter 2 introduces slope change graphs, which illustrate how the slopes for one or more variables change as the weighting procedure changes. The curvatures of these slope change graphs tell one how quickly the slopes change and thus how different the two sets of programs are.

Fifth, if one uses the Generalized Substantive Reweighted Least Squares (GSRLS) version of SWAT, the process diverges a great deal from partitioned regression. That technique, introduced in Chapter 3 and applied in subsequent chapters, reweights the cases after each iteration and thus produces results based on a different final set of exceptional cases. This convergence is a dynamic process that can eventually reveal hidden aspects in the data.

1.7 Don't Throw Away Your Other Tools

SWAT is intended to be one tool in the policy analyst's box of tools. It is not intended to serve as a wholesale substitute for all program evaluation methods. As we note, SWAT is not a technique for estimating parameters (Chapter 2) but rather a qualitative exploratory and prescriptive procedure for isolating performance. Our general approach is to learn as much about our data sets as possible, and this exploration does not need to be limited to estimation of population-wide parameters when prescriptive information is contained in particular cases. Cases of interest stand out as particularly successful or particularly unsuccessful with regard to an analyst-determined measure of performance. As a result, we strongly advocate graphical techniques and the extensive use of regression diagnostics (Hamilton 1992). SWAT and its results mean a lot more to an analyst who is intimately familiar with her data.

We also feel that SWAT is an invaluable tool for structuring additional qualitative analysis. At several points throughout the book, we will illustrate how SWAT not only selects possible cases to study in depth, but also tells the analyst what to look for when examining those cases. Such structured case studies hold out the promise to be an efficient and effective tool in policy analysis.

1.8 When Not to Use SWAT

The use of SWAT should be governed by two rules, one normative and one empirical. The normative rule is simple: if one is interested in programs that do very well or programs that do very poorly or programs that are characterized by some other criterion, then SWAT is a useful approach. Essentially, SWAT is a procedure for incorporating values into statistical analysis. While we feel that policy analysis is inherently interested in values, some analysts may not be interested in values such as performance, equity, risk avoidance, etc., and thus will not be attracted to what SWAT can reveal.

The basic empirical rule of policy analysis is to look at the data, frequently and from different perspectives. Examining distributions and scatterplot matrices can tell one a great deal about policy data and problems that might occur in the analysis (Cleveland 1994, 1993; Hamilton 1992). This has become an essential stage in data exploration and analysis (Hoaglin, Mosteller, and Tukey 1985; Tufte 1990, 1983; Tukey 1977). One especially useful graph in determining whether or not SWAT is useful is the scatterplot of predicted versus actual values from a regression. The graph displays actual performance on the Y-axis and predicted performance based on a vector of X variables on the X-axis (Figure 1.1). We also recommend the use of residual dependence plots where the residuals from a linear regression analysis are plotted against an explanatory variable. These are useful in finding possible heteroscedasticity and correlation between various regressors and the disturbance.

1.8.1 Case 1: No Residual Variation

SWAT is a useful technique when the amount of residual variation is meaningful. Suppose one is looking at average student performance on standardized tests; the standard deviation of the raw data is 10 percentage points and the mean is 60. Furthermore, assume that performance is predicted with a vector of X variables. If the residual variation of the regression equation is too small substantively to be meaningful, then SWAT is unlikely to reveal much useful information. A regression standard error of 1 percentage point, for example, would mean that very little variation in performance is not accounted for by the vector of X variables. The remaining variation is so small that useful information is unlikely to be gained from a SWAT analysis. A graph of such a situation is shown in Figure 1.3, Panel 1. All of the points lie very close to and equidistant from the line.

While a predicted versus actual graph provides a hint that there is not sufficient residual variation for a meaningful SWAT analysis, it is only a hint. The real test is the standard error of the regression. If this error (or plus or minus two times this error) is not a large enough amount of change to matter in terms of public policy, then SWAT is not a useful technique.

1.8.2 Case 2: When There Is a Clear Break Between Two Sets of Programs

Figure 1.3, Panel 2 shows a predicted versus actual graph where one set of agencies is clearly distinct from the other. While SWAT might well work in this situation (if the difference is not absorbed in the intercept), the first step should be to determine

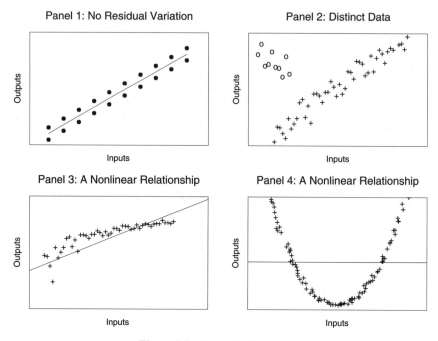

Figure 1.3 Regression Pathologies

what factor or factors distinguish the groups from each other. In this situation one might well have an underspecified model. For example, if these are child support collection programs and most programs in one group use court enforcement to collect support and most in the other group use administrative procedures, then that variable needs to be incorporated into the analysis before SWAT is used. Underspecification is as serious a problem for SWAT as it is for regression.

1.8.3 Case 3: An Incorrect Functional Form

Figure 1.3, Panels 3 and 4 illustrate classic specification errors that occur when an analyst assumes that relationships are linear when they are not. A SWAT analysis on these data will generate misleading results; it will designate some average programs as relatively high performing and consider some programs performing at the highest levels to actually be average or low performers. Note that *the standard linear model would also fail in this circumstance*. The solution is relatively easy: estimate the model in correct functional form and then conduct the SWAT analysis using the output from that equation. In the example provided in Panel 3 of Figure 1.3, the data exhibit a natural logarithmic form, suggesting an exponential transformation to achieve linearity. The shape of the data in Panel 4 of Figure 1.3 suggests the development of a polynomial regression model.

1.9 Plan of the Book

This chapter should be both the first chapter one reads and the last chapter one reads. It introduces the policy analyst to the Zen of SWAT. Doing so before learning any of the techniques is somewhat artificial, however, since many of our suggestions will have meaning only in the context of performing an analysis. The best strategy, we believe, is to read Chapter 1 at the beginning and then return and reread Chapter 1 after mastering the techniques in each chapter. Data sets and software are included with this text. We strongly suggest that the reader use and experiment with the software; SWAT analysis is best learned by experimenting and practicing. Remember that one can "bend" data in many ways, some useful and some not, but one can never "break" the data.

Chapter 2 provides an introduction to SWAT by illustrating the use of the most basic form of SWAT, Substantively Weighted Least Squares (SWLS). The chapter will proceed by walking through the process of a SWLS exercise and introduce the reader to various graphs, summary measures, and individual techniques. This chapter illustrates the basics of SWAT analysis by the development of an actual public policy issue—heterogeneity in success rates for state-level child support programs.

Chapter 3 introduces Generalized Substantively Reweighted Least Squares and the statistical theory behind SWAT analysis and how it deviates from classical linear statistical modeling. It links various decisions by the analyst to known statistical distributions and indicates how the various parameters can be altered to fit the need of the analyst. First-time readers may elect to postpone reading the chapter without reducing their appreciation for subsequent chapters.

Chapter 4 demonstrates how SWAT can incorporate other values into an analysis. Performance-optimizing programs, failed programs, and risk averse programs are examined with SWAT techniques. This chapter provides an excellent opportunity for the reader to see the flexibility of the weighting technique and hopefully stimulate new ideas for her own applications.

Chapter 5 extends this process by manipulating the criterion for "good" performance. By systematically restricting the subset of agencies to those that are more and more distinct from the average, we show the utility of SWAT techniques for the analysis of truly exceptional cases.

Chapter 6 introduces the use of an exogenous variable to establish the weighting process. In this case equity is used as the weight criterion, and the analysis looks at high-performing agencies subject to the constraint of equity. This approach provides another distinct notion of the *substantive* aspect of the SWAT procedure.

Chapter 7 moves into pooled time series analysis to address such questions as organizational stability and consistent high levels of performance. This advanced application of the SWAT procedure is provided to give methodologically interested readers an example of the flexibility of the technique.

Chapter 8 concludes by recapping the central substantive importance of SWAT techniques to the goals of the policy analyst. We argue here that the development of the tools provided in this book should be an indispensable part of the analyst's toolbox of quantitative methods.

1.10 Discussion

This collection of studies is our attempt to reorient the methodological thinking of policy analysts, to get them to focus on what they need to know methodologically. The tool we develop for this is Substantively Weighted Analytical Techniques (SWAT). We make no claims that SWAT is the final word on policy analysis, only that it gives the analyst some different insights from those of traditional linear analysis. The possibilities of developing alternative methods along SWAT lines or some other criteria are endless. By subjecting methodological development to the needs of the analyst, we are trying to get policy analysts to look at their craft from a different perspective.

The distinction that methodological developments should be tailored to specific social science fields is important. Until policy analysts possess and understand a set of appropriate tools, there is always going to be a selection process among the necessarily larger collection of potentially adaptable methods in political science, sociology, economics, and psychology. Furthermore, these fields present a vast cornucopia of tempting treats, only few of which are not poisonous to the policy analysis process.

1.11 References

Amemiya, Takeshi. 1985. *Advanced Econometrics.* Oxford: Blackwell.

Andrews, David F. 1974. "A Robust Method for Multiple Linear Regression." *Technometrics* 16: 523–31.

Anselin, Luc. 1988. *Spatial Econometrics: Methods and Models.* Boston: Kluwer Academic Publishers.

Bartels, Larry M. 1997. "Specification Uncertainty and Model Averaging." *American Journal of Political Science* 41: 641–75.

Box, George E. P., and George C. Tiao. 1992. *Bayesian Inference in Statistical Analysis.* New York: Wiley.

Cleveland, William. 1994. *The Elements of Graphing Data.* Summit, NJ: Hobart Press.

Cleveland, William S. 1993. *Visualizing Data.* Summit, NJ: Hobart Press.

Fahrmeir, Ludwig, and Gerhard Tutz. 1994. *Multivariate Statistical Modelling Based on Generalized Linear Models.* New York: Springer-Verlag.

Gamerman, Dani. 1997. *Markov Chain Monte Carlo.* New York: Chapman & Hall.

Gelman, Andrew, John B. Carlin, Hal S. Stern, and Donald B. Rubin. 1995. *Bayesian Data Analysis.* London: Chapman & Hall.

Greene, William. 1999. *Econometric Analysis.* Fourth edition. New York: Macmillan.

Hamilton, Lawrence C. 1992. *Regression with Graphics.* Pacific Grove, CA: Brooks/Cole.

Hastie, Trevor J., and Robert J. Tibshirani. 1990. *Generalized Additive Models.* New York: Chapman & Hall.

Hoaglin, D. C., Frederick Mosteller, and John Tukey. 1985. *Exploring Data Tables, Trends, and Shapes.* New York: Wiley.

Judge, George G., Tsuong-Chao Lee, and R. Carter Hill. 1985. *Introduction to the Theory and Practice of Econometrics.* New York: Wiley.

McCullagh, P., and J. Nelder. 1983. *Generalized Linear Models.* New York: Chapman & Hall.

Miller, Alan J. 1990. *Subset Selection in Regression.* New York: Chapman & Hall.

Miller, Alan J. 1984. "Selection of Subsets of Regression Variables." *Journal of the Royal Statistical Society A* 147: 389–425.

Rousseeuw, Peter J., and Annick M. Leroy. 1987. *Robust Regression and Outlier Detection.* New York: Wiley.

Scott, David W. 1992. *Multivariate Density Estimation: Theory, Practice, and Visualization.* New York: Wiley.

Simon, Herbert. 1969. *The Sciences of the Artificial.* Cambridge, MA: MIT Press.

Tanner, Martin. 1996. *Tools for Statistical Inference: Methods for the Exploration of Posterior Distributions and Likelihood Functions.* New York: Springer-Verlag.

Tufte, Edward R. 1990. *Envisioning Information.* Cheshire, CT: Graphics Press.

Tufte, Edward R. 1983. *The Visual Display of Quantitative Information.* Cheshire, CT: Graphics Press.

Tukey, John W. 1977. *Exploratory Data Analysis.* Reading, MA: Addison-Wesley.

Chapter 2

An Introduction to Substantively Weighted Least Squares[1]

Kenneth J. Meier, Jeff Gill, Lael R. Keiser

2.1 Introduction

The policy analysis concern with how things might be (rather than how things are) is not so different from Max Weber's (1946) emphasis on the ideal type: both are seeking to illustrate or obtain some optimum level of performance. Consistent with these values, many believe that sciences of the artificial should focus on finding ways to improve system performance rather than seeking purely theoretical knowledge. This orientation is prevalent in public administration, policy analysis, and most of the social sciences. In public administration these different views of research are part of the chasm that separates academics from practitioners in the

---

[1] A previous version of this chapter appeared as Kenneth J. Meier and Lael R. Keiser. 1996. "Public Administration as a Science of the Artificial: A Methodology for Prescription." *Public Administration Review* 56: 459–66. Larry Bartels, Gary King, Bert Kritzer, and three anonymous reviewers provided helpful comments on that manuscript. Inspiration for the paper came from Bartels (1996), who proposed the use of weighting to determine whether groups of different cases should be pooled, and Kritzer (1996), who proposed that we should play with data like musicians play with a score, stretching the limits of what the score can do.

field. Academics, while occasionally finding results with practical applications, focus on how things are, on the empirical description of the administrative world. Scholarly journals reinforce that emphasis. Practitioners, in contrast, seek to know what is possible in an applied setting.

This chapter shows that at partial fault for the separation between academics and practitioners is the dominant methodology used by both scholars and practitioners—linear regression-based techniques. Regression methods by their very nature tend to downplay the unusual and focus on the typical cases. Recent developments in regression diagnostics (Belsley, Kuh, and Welsch 1980; Rousseeuw and Leroy 1987), though rarely used in public administration or public policy, downplay the unusual cases even more. As a result, although these techniques add useful information, they will increase the academic–practitioner gap. The second portion of this chapter introduces substantively weighted least squares (SWLS), a SWAT technique that has the potential to transform the basic quantitative method of policy analysis and public administration (regression) from a tool that explains *what is* to a tool that can be used to search for *what might be*.

We illustrate our method with an analysis of child support enforcement at the state level. The key question driving that research is, why do some organizations learn to perform their functions at a faster rate than others do? Our argument will first introduce the substantive case, child support enforcement, and briefly present the regression findings of a traditional study. We will then introduce some techniques of resistant and robust regression and argue that these methods take public managers in a completely wrong direction. We will illustrate substantively weighted least squares, a technique that puts more weight on the highest-performing agencies. The method shows that some variables may be far more important for effective performance than normal linear regression techniques demonstrate.

2.2 Child Support Enforcement

In 1975 the federal government required that state governments set up procedures to compel absent parents to support their dependent children. Although some states had long operated such programs, many did not. In the past 20 years, all states have gained substantial experience operating these programs, and academic research has discovered some effective collection techniques (Klawitter and Garfinkel 1991; Michalopoulas and Garfinkel 1989). The relative effectiveness of these programs, however, varies a great deal. In 1991, Michigan collected about seventy-four dollars per capita in child support while Arizona was able to collect only nine dollars per capita. Although this state-to-state variation is an interesting topic in and of itself (Keiser, 1996), our concern is with how well these agencies have improved their performance over time, something that we term "organizational learning."

To measure learning, we took child support collections (per 1000 population) in constant dollars for all years from 1982 to 1991 (see the chapter addendum, Section 2.11, for sources of these data).[2] We plotted these data and ran 50 linear regressions. The slope coefficients from these models indicate the annual average improvement in real dollars collected per 1000 population.

2.3 The Original Study

In any SWAT analysis, the first step is to create a model where the policy output is a function of various explanatory inputs, some of which are hopefully controllable by public managers. Seven variables were hypothesized to affect organization learning by the child support bureaucracy.[3] These can be divided into three types—support by advocates, subject characteristics, and bureaucratic capacity. Support by advocates should increase learning because it provides pressure on the bureaucracy to improve, as well as provides legitimacy for the bureaucracy's function (Sabatier and Jenkins-Smith 1993). To measure advocate support, the number of chapters in each state of the Association for Children for Enforcement of Support (ACES) per million population was included in the model. ACES is the only client-based organization focused directly on child support enforcement (see Keiser, 1996).

Subject characteristics, that is, the nature of the bureaucracy's inputs, should also affect learning rates (Lebovic 1995). Three subject characteristics are of interest here—instability, ambiguity, and levels of demand. Instability in the workload refers to high rates of change in caseload numbers. Instability may facilitate learning because it puts pressure on the bureaucracy to innovate to deal with its changing environment. The standard deviation of the child support bureaucracy's annual caseload measures this type of instability.

Similarly to instability, ambiguity or heterogeneity, the mix in the type of cases the bureaucracy must deal with, may increase learning by increasing the innovation needed to deal with the different types of cases (for an alternate view see Mazmanian and Sabatier 1989). Child support agencies deal with two types of clients—those who receive welfare payments, a program at the time called Aid to Families with Dependent Children (AFDC), and those who do not. For AFDC clients, whether or not the noncustodial parent has the income to support the

---

[2]We could have created a reasonably similar measure by simply subtracting 1982 collections from 1991 collections. The disadvantage of this simpler method is that it relies on only two of the ten years to calculate a measure of change. If either one of these years is unusual for any reason, the change measure will be biased. The use of a regression slope is simply a way to get more information into the calculation of the change measure.

[3]Readers interested in the substantive issues addressed here, including alternative specifications, are referred to the in-depth discussion in Keiser (1996).

children is open to question (Alfasso and Chakmakas 1983; McDonald and Moran 1983). For a variety of reasons, AFDC cases are more difficult to resolve than non-AFDC cases. The percentage of agency cases that are for AFDC clients (measured as an average from 1982 to 1991) is our measure of heterogeneity/ambiguity.

The level of demand should also influence learning. More clients for the bureaucracy should increase the visibility of the problem and make it more likely that the bureaucracy will feel pressure to step up its activity. We measure this potential level of demand by the state's divorce rate. An increase in divorces generates additional cases for child support enforcement.

Finally, bureaucratic capacity should also affect learning. Changes in personnel resources, organizational slack, and bureaucratic monetary resources should all influence how fast the bureaucracy learns. On the one hand, learning should be enhanced if an organization has ample resources since these can be devoted to experimentation or greater investment in the human resources skills of the agency. Against this logic is the notion that necessity is the mother of invention. Agencies will learn faster if they are forced to do so because they lack the resources to do their current job. The measures are the change in agency personnel (1982 to 1991) per million population, the change in agency budgets (1982 to 1991) per thousand population, and the 1982–1991 change in agency slack (defined as the number of employees per 1000 active cases).

The results of an ordinary least squares regression analysis are shown in Table 2.1. We believe that null hypothesis significance testing as performed in the social and applied sciences suffers from a wide range of serious problems (Gill 1999; see also our preface). As a result we will report 95% confidence intervals for estimated coefficients rather than specific p-values. It is important to know that a 95% confidence interval that is bounded away from zero is functionally equivalent to a p-value that is less than 0.05. However, reporting confidence intervals avoids pathologies such as null hypothesis confirmation, replication fallacies, and mistaken inverse probability interpretation associated with p-values and "stars."

These findings reveal that learning is a function of both internal and external factors of the organization. Of the external factors, only political support (ACES chapters) has a strong positive impact on organizational learning: it is the only confidence interval among the external factors that does not include zero.

Internally, factors that have coefficient estimates with 95% confidence intervals bounded away from zero are expenditures and personnel; agencies with larger budgets are able to increase their collections at a faster rate than other agencies, and agencies that have a greater increase in employees also are able to improve their collection rates. Although it has a coefficient estimate with a 95% confidence interval covering zero, organizational slack is still worth looking at. The negative coefficient supports the necessity view of learning: as organizational slack decreases, the organization is more likely to learn. Although these findings are

2 An Introduction to Substantively Weighted Least Squares 21

Table 2.1 Determinants of Organizational Learning

	Explanatory Variable	Slope	Std. Error	95% CI
	Intercept	−263.508	591.866	[−1423.565: 896.549]
Support by Advocates	ACES Chapters per million	284.795	99.831	[89.126: 480.464]
Subject Characteristics	Work Load Instability (×100)	0.382	0.206	[−0.022: 0.786]
	Work Load Ambiguity	9.004	11.259	[−13.064: 31.072]
	Average Divorce Rate	−1.682	14.412	[−29.930: 26.566]
Bureaucratic Capacity	Staff Change per million	4.617	1.758	[1.171: 8.063]
	Average Organization Slack	−125.335	88.330	[−298.462: 47.792]
	Average Expenditure	0.294	0.078	[0.141: 0.447]

Adjusted $R^2 = 0.36$
$F = 5.00$ on 7 and 42 degrees of freedom
Residual Standard Error = 649.34

interesting in and of themselves, they are introduced merely to illustrate the potential hazards of recent developments in regression diagnostics and to set up the application of the SWLS.

2.4 Regression Diagnostics

Linear regression analysis has many limitations. It relies on the principle of minimizing squared error to fit a regression line to a set of data. Squared error rather than average error or some other criterion was originally chosen because it permitted relatively easy derivation of formulae to use in calculation, and it leads to some very elegant theory (Gauss–Markov). This ease was not without a downside, which can best be illustrated by reference to Table 2.2.

Table 2.2 shows the actual values of learning for each of the 50 state programs. Since these numbers represent changes in dollars collected per year per 1000 people, they might best be understood by dividing them by 1000. For example, the state of Alabama was able to increase child support collections by $1.14 per person per year from 1982 to 1991 (in constant dollars). The predicted value is the value that the regression equation predicts based on the explanatory variables. The residual is the amount by which the prediction misses the actual value. In other words, Alabama improved its collections by 0.56 (56 cents) less per person per year than would be expected for a state with its ACES membership, workload stability, workload ambiguity, divorce rate, expenditures, change in staff, and organizational slack. This information is useful to both the analyst and the practitioner. If one wants to visit a state agency that is performing much better than expected to see how they do it, then Wisconsin (residual 2001) and Ohio (1552) are the places to visit; one would avoid California (−1134) and New York (−1195).

Kenneth J. Meier, Jeff Gill, Lael R. Keiser

Table 2.2 Measures of Learning and Regression Statistics

State	Actual	Predicted	Residual	R Student	Cook's D
Alabama	1141.40	1701.27	−559.87	−0.88	0.01
Alaska	2667.00	2686.00	−19.00	−0.04	0.00
Arizona	307.30	899.98	−592.68	−1.01	0.03
Arkansas	840.70	405.43	435.27	0.71	0.01
California	482.50	1616.03	−1133.53	−1.85	0.03
Colorado	550.00	1206.39	−656.39	−1.05	0.01
Connecticut	514.10	1063.84	−549.74	−0.91	0.02
Delaware	**1352.50**	**265.74**	**1086.76**	**2.46**	**0.63**
Florida	1136.50	1305.75	−169.25	−0.28	0.00
Georgia	1575.40	1684.74	−109.34	−0.17	0.00
Hawaii	1170.60	894.75	275.85	0.44	0.00
Idaho	1679.60	1117.57	562.03	0.89	0.01
Illinois	882.30	1595.19	−712.89	−1.27	0.06
Indiana	1347.50	1054.20	293.30	0.49	0.01
Iowa	1353.40	1056.56	296.84	0.47	0.00
Kansas	1363.40	1578.92	−215.52	−0.34	0.00
Kentucky	1087.90	1577.76	−489.86	−0.79	0.01
Louisiana	712.80	840.12	−127.32	−0.20	0.00
Maine	1865.40	1817.79	47.61	0.08	0.00
Maryland	1088.40	1808.84	−720.44	−1.18	0.02
Massachusetts	1308.10	1804.85	−496.75	−0.79	0.01
Michigan	3485.40	2774.67	710.73	1.27	0.07
Minnesota	1946.40	1668.86	277.54	0.44	0.00
Mississippi	1116.80	1458.63	−341.83	−0.61	0.02
Missouri	2047.50	1285.14	762.36	1.21	0.01
Montana	893.30	1146.50	−253.20	−0.41	0.00
Nebraska	1779.20	1314.55	464.65	0.78	0.01
Nevada	703.40	767.32	−63.92	−0.15	0.00
New Hampshire	695.10	1125.70	−430.60	−0.76	0.02
New Jersey	1287.00	1726.65	−439.65	−0.72	0.01
New Mexico	573.00	746.92	−173.92	−0.28	0.00
New York	955.60	2150.63	−1195.03	−2.08	0.09
North Carolina	1296.10	1117.27	178.83	0.28	0.00
North Dakota	1194.50	1008.37	186.13	0.30	0.00
Ohio	**4299.20**	**2747.62**	**1551.58**	**3.16**	**0.46**
Oklahoma	896.40	934.48	−38.08	−0.06	0.00
Oregon	815.40	1037.41	−222.01	−0.42	0.01
Pennsylvania	2262.90	1788.24	474.66	0.81	0.02
Rhode Island	1108.80	1162.17	−53.37	−0.09	0.00
South Carolina	1314.20	1179.20	135.00	0.22	0.00
South Dakota	1268.90	1497.60	−228.70	−0.40	0.01
Tennessee	952.80	1162.03	−209.23	−0.35	0.00
Texas	763.20	1122.87	−359.67	−0.64	0.02
Utah	1228.60	1183.37	45.23	0.07	0.00
Vermont	1023.50	1636.61	−613.11	−1.04	0.03
Virginia	1646.30	1493.20	153.10	0.24	0.00
Washington	2483.30	2369.55	113.75	0.20	0.00
West Virginia	1045.30	593.00	452.30	0.73	0.01
Wisconsin	**3866.90**	**1866.00**	**2000.90**	**3.61**	**0.08**
Wyoming	1450.20	779.73	670.47	1.13	0.03

The column labeled "*R* Student" provides the jackknifed or externally Studentized residuals:[4] a measure of how far off the predictions of the regression are for that case in standardized units (see Chapter 3; or Rousseeuw and Leroy 1987, p. 226; Hamilton 1992, p. 132). A jackknifed residual can be used as an indication that a case is problematic in a given model. Minimizing squared error essentially means that a hypothetical case which is a distance of 2 units from the fitted regression line (its residual) now counts 4 times as much as a case that is only 1 unit from the fitted line. If such a case has the right characteristics, it can distort the regression line and produce misleading results. Since they are in standardized units, these jackknifed residuals can be used to designate cases that potentially distort a regression. The general rule of thumb is that cases with jackknifed residuals greater than 2 or less than -2 should be examined (the distribution is asymptotically t).

Whether a case with a large jackknifed residual actually distorts the regression line depends on the individual case. In this case, if the agency is fairly similar to all other agencies in terms of the values on the explanatory variables, then it will have little influence on the overall regression. If the case is unusual relative to other cases, then it is more likely to distort the regression. Statisticians have developed several measures of this distortion; Table 2.2 reports such a measure, Cook's D, which is a measure of how much the regression slopes change when that individual case is dropped from the regression (Hamilton 1992, p. 132; Rousseeuw and Leroy 1987, pp. 227–8). A glance at the table reveals that Wisconsin has the largest residual (R Student $= 3.61$) but has virtually no influence on the regression line (Cook's $D = 0.08$). Both Ohio and Delaware have smaller residuals but exert greater influence on the overall regression (OH $R = 3.16$, $D = 0.46$; DE $R = 2.46$, $D = 0.63$).[5]

Figure 2.1 graphically demonstrates the difference that can exist between the jackknifed residual's size and the Cook's distance. This is a two-panel index plot where the first panel depicts the magnitude of the 50 Studentized residuals (alphabetically) and the second plot depicts the magnitude of the 50 Cook's distances (also alphabetically so they line up vertically). Note the visual support for the difference between residual size for Delaware and Ohio versus Wisconsin. Sometimes it is the case that points with great influence have small residuals because they "pull" the line (plane, or hyperplane) towards their position. In this case, however, Delaware and Ohio have both large influence *and* large residuals.

---

[4]The given value is $t_{(i)} = \dfrac{R_i}{s_{(i)}\sqrt{1-h_{ii}}}$ where R_i is the ith residual from the linear model, $s_{(i)}$ is the standard error when the ith case is omitted, and h_{ii} is the ith diagonal of the hat matrix.

[5]The rule of thumb is that cases are influential if the Cook's D exceeds $4/n$, where n is the number of cases; in this example that would be 0.08. So technically Wisconsin does have some influence, but it is relatively minor compared to the Ohio and Delaware cases.

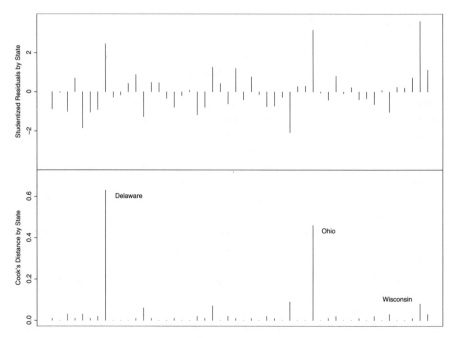

Figure 2.1 Residuals and Influence Index Plot

To illustrate the impact that just a single case can have on a regression line, let us take the case of Delaware. The unusual variable for Delaware is the change in staff. Although the average agency increased its staffing by 55 persons per million population, Delaware actually reduced overall staff by 232 persons per million. If they had actually cut staff at twice that rate, the regression coefficient for staff for the entire equation would have dropped 49% from 4.617 to 2.24 and would have become statistically insignificant (a 95% confidence interval covering zero). Alternatively, if Delaware simply kept staffing the same size as before, the regression slope for staff would have increased 42% to 6.553, and the slope for slack would have increased about one-third and become statistically significant (a 95% confidence interval bounded away from zero). This illustrates that modest changes in values for individual variables can have a major influence on the results of a regression under the right circumstances.

2.5 Robust and Resistant Regression

At this point it is important to clarify the distinction between robust and resistant techniques. Resistant techniques are those designed to be relatively insensitive to a small number of highly influential values. These values are often large outliers—data points that are atypically distant from the other data points in the context of the specified model. Robust techniques are those designed to be relatively insensitive to deviations from their underlying assumptions. For example, the central limit theorem states that given a reasonable set of conditions, including independence of the data points, the mean is asymptotically normal. However, this property is relatively robust to mild deviations from independence (a fact exploited in the analysis of Markov Chain Monte Carlo results). In contrast, this mean is *not* a particularly resistant technique in that a few extremely large values will substantially alter the subsequent calculation.

Some confusion about the distinction between robustness and resistance stems from the concern of some authors about making the linear model more resistant to highly influential values, and the concern of other authors about making the linear model more robust to deviations from the underlying Gauss–Markov assumptions. Since one of the Gauss–Markov assumptions states that there not be a correlation between some regressor value, X_i, and its corresponding residual, ϵ_i (or any other for that matter), then making the linear model robust to this assumption can also make it resistant to outliers in general.

Recent work in linear models has focused a great deal of attention on diagnostics and the ability of individual cases to distort the results of regressions. An excellent summary of early research on regression diagnostics in this area can be found in Emerson and Hoaglin (1983). A good applied text is Hamilton (1992). Other useful works include Cook and Weisberg (1982), Carroll and Ruppert (1988), Birkes and Dodge (1993), Barnett and Lewis (1978), and Andrews et al. (1972).

Work in this area is motivated by the above mentioned sensitivity of the mean to extreme outliers because the least squares estimates are built upon estimates of means of the explanatory and outcome variables (Chapter 3 provides the applicable derivations). The mean has a *breakdown bound* of zero, meaning that zero percent of the data points can become unbounded (become exceptionally large or go to infinity) before the statistic becomes unbounded (i.e., breaks down). Conversely, the median has a breakdown bound of 0.50 because almost 50 percent of the data points can become unbounded before the median becomes unbounded. The fundamental work on breakdown bounds can be found in Hampel (1974) and Huber (1981).

Resistant regression techniques have been developed to ameliorate the problem of highly influential and sometimes disastrous outliers (Western 1995; Hamilton 1992; Rousseeuw and Leroy 1987; Hoaglin, Mosteller, and Tukey 1983). Essentially the approach taken by several alternative forms of linear regression is based on the idea that summed squared error is not the only function that can be minimized. Edgeworth (1883) is generally credited with the first modern development (Legendre considered but did not fully develop the idea) of minimizing the absolute residuals rather than squared residuals since squaring only makes extreme values all the more extreme. This approach, now called L_1 regression, unfortunately still possesses a breakdown bound of zero.

A broad class of robust regression techniques segment the data points and treat the points in the outer segments differently. The roughest version is alpha-trimming, in which an arbitrary proportion of the data points are simply removed from the analysis (Andrews et al. 1972). A more sophisticated perspective is to take the points in the outer segments and weight them or use a resistant point estimate such as the median within these segments while continuing to use the standard linear model for the well-behaved middle segment. Obviously these approaches require quite a bit of creativity and experimentation of the analyst.

The Huber M-estimator is one of the first rigorous attempts to develop a wide class of robust criteria for producing a linear fit to data (Huber 1973). The idea is to minimize some function of the summed residuals, $\sum f(e_i)$, such that f is a symmetric convex function centered at zero. Therefore, differentiation with respect to the linear model coefficients, β_i, and setting the result equal to zero provides a basis for a class of functions that can be used to calculate regression coefficients that are robust to outliers in the y dimension. Unfortunately, the breakdown bound in any of the x dimensions is still zero. This is, however, a substantial improvement since a regression equation that breaks down in an x direction simply implies no relationship for that variable (i.e., a flat slope), whereas a regression equation that breaks down in the y direction produces slope values equal to infinity and is literally useless in every sense. There is a great deal of work to improve the sensitivity of M-estimators to outliers in an x direction, and these are generally referred to as generalized M-estimators (Krasker 1980; Hampel et al. 1986).

Many robust resistant techniques systematically reduce the influence of the extreme cases by weighting them less in the overall regression. In this very general class of robust regression techniques, selection of the weighting criterion often depends on the structure of the data (Western 1995). One example is given by Andrews (1974); it is relatively effective regardless of the data distribution and, when the data fit a multivariate normal distribution, it produce estimates equal to ordinary least squares. It is an iterative procedure that gradually changes weights until the regression coefficients converge. As an example of robust regression methods, we apply this technique to the data on child support, iterating three times.

Table 2.3 shows the results of robust regression for the child support data set. Both statistically and substantively, the results of Table 2.3 differ from those of Table 2.1. Although ACES chapters retains a 95% confidence interval bounded away from zero, its size (and thus the impact of the variable) drops by about 37%. Staffing changes remain 95% confidence interval bounded away from zero, but again their overall impact drops by about 19%. Expenditures remain positively related to learning and change only moderately (+4%). The most important difference is that slack is now 95% confidence interval bounded away from zero and

2 An Introduction to Substantively Weighted Least Squares 27

Table 2.3   Andrews Robust Regression Results

	Explanatory Variable	Slope	Std. Error	95% CI
	Intercept	101.230	341.780	[−568.659: 771.119]
Support by Advocates	ACES Chapters per million	179.912	61.722	[58.937: 300.887]
Subject Characteristics	Work Load Instability ($\times 100$)	0.233	0.142	[−0.045: 0.511]
	Work Load Ambiguity	4.762	6.603	[−8.180: 17.704]
	Average Divorce Rate	2.220	8.075	[−13.607: 18.047]
Bureaucratic Capacity	Staff Change per million	3.744	1.122	[1.545: 5.943]
	Average Organization Slack	−174.228	52.877	[−277.867:−70.589]
	Average Expenditure	0.306	0.046	[0.216: 0.396]

Adjusted $R^2 = 0.53$

$F = 8.89$ on 7 and 42 degrees of freedom

Residual Standard Error $= 338.77$

has increased its negative impact on learning by 39%. Faced with such findings, an analyst could well advise an agency that greater performance could be obtained by increasing resources but only by increasing them at a rate much slower than workload increases and thus reducing any organizational slack.

Despite the wide endorsement of robust and resistant regression, we feel that, if used uncritically, these may be inappropriate for public policy analysis. Adopting such techniques is the philosophical equivalent of saying that one would like to improve organization performance by looking at what the average agencies are doing. Agencies that are doing better than average relative to their inputs (and those doing worse than average) are systematically downweighted in the regression. By analogy, we might ask Swiss Rail to study Amtrak, or the U.S. Postal Service to adopt the tactics of the Italian PTT (Post, Telephone, and Telegraph). Such a strategy might well pay off for agencies that are poor performers, but it holds no benefits for those agencies that are doing well. This strategy is essentially what academic research using regression has been recommending to practitioners. As the quality of regression skills improves and regression diagnostics and robust regression enter public administration and public policy, academic research could become even less valuable for practicing public administrators. The concern in policy analysis is not to get average performance out of an agency given the level of resources that it gets, but to get above average performance for those resources.

2.6 SWLS

With some adjustment, however, regression analysis can be converted to a new tool for both academics and practitioners. In public policy we should be interested in the high-performing programs and what they can tell us relative to those programs that do not do so well. From Table 2.2 we are interested in those with positive residuals, those whose learning curve grew faster than we would have expected given their environment and internal factors. As an initial rule of thumb, we propose that cases with a jackknifed residual of +0.7 or more be designated as the high-performing cases (see Chapter 3 where this threshold is generalized to any value that the researcher sees as valuable). This criterion will generally designate about 20 percent of the cases as high-performing[6] with this particular data set.

Rather than weighting these high-performing agencies less (as robust regression would do), one should weight them relatively more than average or low-performing agencies. Our technique is to rerun the regression equations using weighted least squares. In the first run we weight the "average cases" (that is, those with Studentized residuals of less than 0.7) to count as 0.9 case and leave the high-performing cases as they are. We consecutively run nine regressions, each time reducing the weight on the "average cases" by 0.1 until the final regression weights the high-performing agencies at 1.0 and the average performers at 0.1. These regressions gradually give relatively more weight to the higher-performing agencies, and in the process the analyst can see how the slopes change to indicate what the high-performing agencies do that the typical ones do not (shown in Table 2.6 below).

SWLS and other SWAT techniques do not estimate population parameters; that is, there is no longer a population to make inferences about. SWLS slopes should be thought of as indicators of how some agencies are different. Because SWAT regressions resemble linear regression models, we will retain the standard terminology (slope, intercept, standard error) to avoid confusion. The coefficients are qualitative indicators of roughly how much more (or less) high-performing bureaucracies may get from their individual inputs.

Before performing SWLS, the analyst should always examine the means for all explanatory variables for both the average and the high-performing programs. The analyst needs to determine whether the programs are relatively similar in terms of inputs so that the different results are not just a function of differences in program resources.

Table 2.4 shows the means for both sets of programs; in no case is the mean for the high-performing programs statistically different from that of the average programs at any commonly used alpha value. This is shown in Figure 2.2 where the average-performing and high-performing 95% confidence intervals are compared for each variable. The difference between the average and the high-performing programs is in what they do with the resources that they get, not in the amount of resources available.

---

[6]The number of cases is a trade-off. The fewer the number that are designated, the more the outcome will be the result of one or two cases which may or may not be generalizable. The analyst wants sufficient cases to be able to say that the relationships hold in a lot of agencies but not so many cases that one generalizes to the mediocre cases. See Chapter 5.

Table 2.4 Comparison of Average and High-Performing Programs

	Explanatory Variable	Average Cases Mean	Average Cases Std. Error	High-Performing Cases Mean	High-Performing Cases Std. Error
Support by Advocates	ACES Chapters per million	0.93	1.01	1.36	1.03
Subject Characteristics	Work Load Instability	63,122.61	69,454.84	49,166.06	44,234.76
	Work Load Ambiguity	29.76	16.91	27.65	9.97
	Average Divorce Rate	21.48	5.41	21.78	7.38
Bureaucratic Capacity	Staff Change per million	57.78	104.39	55.05	61.55
	Average Organization Slack	3.61	1.94	3.65	1.35
	Average Expenditure	3633.50	1371.74	3613.08	1471.29

The second step in SWLS is to plot the data and determine whether the pattern violates any of the warning signs noted in Chapter 1. Two recommended plots are the scatterplot of the predicted versus actual learning for these agencies, Panel 1 of Figure 2.3, and a residual dependence plot by the order of the fitted estimate of the outcome variable, Panel 2 of Figure 2.3. The residual dependence plot is fitted with confidence bands corresponding to the number of standard deviations away from zero. For instance, the second darkest band contains points that are at least two standard deviations away from zero and therefore less than 5% likely under the normal theory assumptions that support the linear regression model.

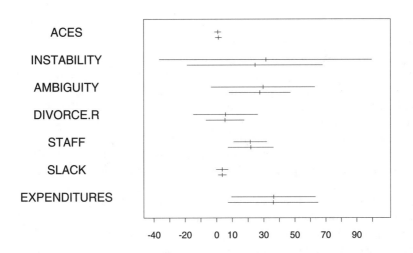

95% Confidence Intervals, Average Performers over High Performers

Tick marks at the mean, Instability, Divorce Rate, and Expenditures Scaled to Fit

Figure 2.2 95% Confidence Interval Comparisons

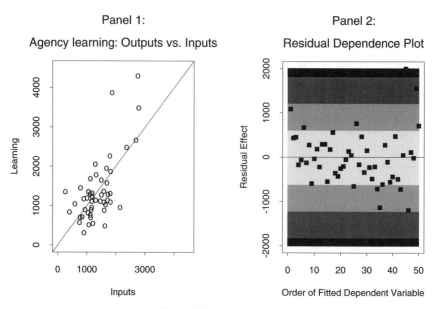

Figure 2.3 Linear Model

Neither plot reveals problems. Although there might be a slight nonlinear relationship in the data in the upper extremity, the data appear to have sufficient variance after the regression to perform SWLS. The analyst should then examine the standard error of the regression (649.34 reported in Table 2.1). The original learning variable had a mean of 1376 and a standard deviation of 813. The standard error of the regression suggests that substantial variation in performance remains unexplained. Plus or minus two standard deviations would translate to ±$1300 in child support collections per year per 1000 people, an amount that is substantively well worth examining in detail.

Table 2.5 reports the change in slope coefficients for five of the explanatory variables—ACES, instability, staff, slack, and expenditures. All slopes are divided by the ordinary least squares (OLS) slope so that changes can be compared in percentage terms to the linear model and to each other. The other two variables are omitted because they were not 95% confidence interval bounded away from zero or close to it in either the original regression or in the robust regression. The final row of Table 2.5 shows how much the coefficients changed when the

2 An Introduction to Substantively Weighted Least Squares   31

Table 2.5   Change in Slope Coefficients with Iterative Weighting

Weight	ACES	Instability	Staff	Slack	Expenditures
1.0	1.000	1.000	1.000	1.000	1.000
0.9	1.003	1.053	1.002	0.973	1.004
0.8	1.007	1.112	1.003	0.939	1.008
0.7	1.010	1.178	1.005	0.896	1.013
0.6	1.012	1.253	1.008	0.842	1.019
0.5	1.015	1.339	1.012	0.770	1.025
0.4	1.019	1.437	1.019	0.672	1.034
0.3	1.029	1.545	1.033	0.531	1.047
0.2	1.059	1.649	1.068	0.316	1.075
0.1	1.172	1.654	1.179	−0.045	1.162

Figures are SWLS slopes divided by OLS slopes.

high-performing agencies were weighted ten times that of the average agencies.[7] The actual regression coefficients for the last run are reported in Table 2.6.

One graphical method of presenting SWLS results is the slope change graph. Figure 2.4, the slope change graph, essentially plots the values in Table 2.5 against the weights used in the regression. This allows the analyst to observe how the individual slopes change as the weighting process occurs. In Figure 2.4 we can easily note the distinguishing effects of instability and slack. Slack clearly declines

Table 2.6   Organizational Learning: The Ideal Regression

	Explanatory Variable	Slope	Std. Error	95% CI	
	Intercept	4.187	877.228	[−171932.500:	171940.900]
Support by Advocates	ACES Chapters per million	333.752	117.107	[104.222:	563.282]
Subject Characteristics	Work Load Instability*	0.631	0.242	[0.157:	1.105]
	Work Load Ambiguity	−0.572	11.657	[−23.420:	22.276]
	Average Divorce Rate	−16.887	21.001	[−58.049:	24.275]
Bureaucratic Capacity	Staff Change per million	5.445	2.248	[1.039:	9.851]
	Average Organization Slack	5.579	117.953	[−225.609:	236.767]
	Average Expenditure	0.342	0.107	[0.132:	0.552]

Adjusted $R^2 = 0.63$
$F = 12.93$ on 7 and 42 degrees of freedom
Residual Standard Error $= 367.06$
*Coefficient multiplied by 100 to facilitate comparison

---

[7]This is not as extreme as it sounds since there are four times as many average agencies. The high performers as a group, therefore, are weighted to contribute about 2.5 times what the average performers contribute to the regression as a group.

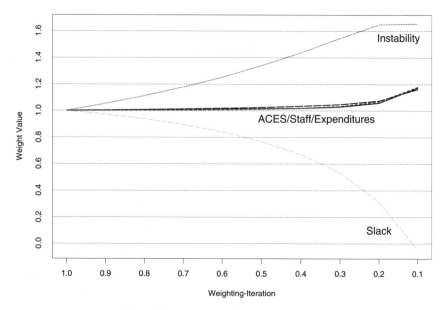

Figure 2.4 Slope Changes vs Weight Changes

in importance as the weights incrementally favor high-performing agencies. Conversely, instability increases in importance to these same agencies.

The multiregression barplot (Figure 2.5) is a visual way to compare the OLS and the final SWLS regression. The sizes of the coefficients are represented by the heights of the bars, according to the Y-axis scale, whereas the shading reveals the level of statistical significance (p-values used here for visual convenience only). The barplot presents at a glance the differences between the linear model (OLS derived estimates) and SWLS. It is important to note that horizontal (within-model) comparisons are not valid as each of the variables is measured in different units. The purpose of the multiregression barplot is to vertically compare the effect of the *same* variable in different models. Previously, readers were forced to flip between different tables (typically on different pages) and get an idea of relative importance from the numerical values.

Some of the SWLS results are simply incremental changes. The slopes for ACES, staff, and expenditures increase 17%, 18%, and 16%, respectively. Since these figures are still held down somewhat by the average cases, we might think of these as indicating a minimum level of distinction between the high-performing programs and the rest. Substantively this implies that higher-performing child support programs get about 17% more learning from ACES political support, 18% more learning from additions to staff, and 16% more learning from increases to

2 An Introduction to Substantively Weighted Least Squares   33

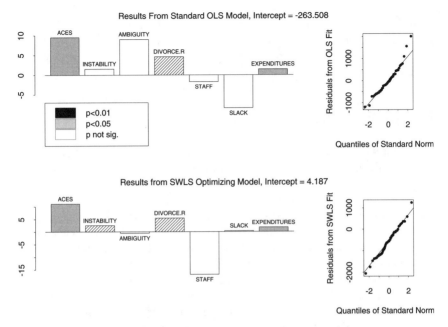

Figure 2.5   Multiregression Barplot

expenditures, all other things being equal. Although these are not gigantic differences, they are worth investigating. Any program that can increase its performance by 18% more for a staff increase than a similar program can is clearly doing something worthwhile. Exactly what, can be determined by in-depth case analysis of these programs focusing on staff-related variables.

The real differences, however, are for instability and organizational slack. The high-performing programs clearly take better advantage of the instability in their environment; the slope for instability increases by 65%. If one were looking for major performance payoffs, these programs should be examined for how they manage and adapt to workload fluctuations. During that process, practitioners might find the important factors that separate high-performing child support collection programs from mediocre ones. Equally striking is the relationship for organizational slack. While robust regression told us that slack was important to learning, the SWLS shows that slack affects the performance of only the average programs. Not only does it have little impact on the high-performing programs, but its impact actually drops to zero. High-performing child support enforcement programs appear to be simply unaffected by the amount of slack resources in the organization. Therein lies the danger of even the best-informed regression techniques.

The robust regression results would have encouraged practitioners to keep organizational slack as limited as possible to encourage better program performance. This advice is bad; organizational slack by itself has no impact on organizational learning among programs that learn the most quickly.

2.7 Some Caveats

We do not wish to imply that scholars should abandon ordinary least squares or regression diagnostics; they are obviously valuable research skills. Ordinary least squares and robust regression are the preferred techniques to generalize from a sample to a population. They demonstrate how things are. Neither SWLS nor other SWAT techniques can be used to estimate relationships for a group of agencies; they are techniques used for performance isolation and recommendation—qualitative techniques that demonstrate how things might be. Both forms of analysis should be used and the results from both presented to the reader.

Although we have illustrated substantively weighted least squares here as a specific technique when applied to regression analysis, in reality SWAT is a general quantitative tool. The basic principle of emphasizing certain types of cases can be used in conjunction with statistical methods other than regression.

2.8 SWAT Versus Best Practices

Although SWAT may superficially seem much like the best practices literature, they are significantly different. The best practices literature seeks out high-performing organizations and attempts to find techniques in those organizations that can be transferred to other organizations (Osborne and Gaebler 1992). Although both approaches focus on high-performing agencies, SWAT avoids the pitfalls of the best practices literature (see Overman and Boyd 1994).

First, because SWAT relies on regression and the need for comparable data, it forces the analyst to compare agencies that are performing the same task. The risk of applying inappropriate private sector techniques to public sector problems is avoided. Second, SWAT does not rely on a subjective selection of the ideal case (Overman and Boyd 1994, p. 69); SWAT defines optimum cases as those that perform better than expected given the variables that influence performance. Within a regression context, the subset of cases is highly constrained. High performers in SWAT analyses are based on objective measures of performance. Third, whereas best practices is applications driven, SWAT is clearly research driven. This distinction will provide a restraint on the "hero worship" tone that characterizes some of the best practices literature (Lynn 1987). Fourth, the best practices literature is positive and prescriptive while our technique is prescriptive but may well not be positive. That is, our technique is not inherently optimistic; the key variables discovered might well be beyond control of management (see Chapter 4). Finally, while the best practices research is not theory-testing research (Overman and Boyd 1994, p. 79), our approach starts with an effort to test theory and find relationships and only then shifts to prescription.

2.9 SWAT Versus L-Regression: A Methodological Interlude

In classical linear regression a desirable property of regression estimators is that they should be relatively insensitive to large outliers. Since the ordinary least squares estimation procedure that underlies the linear model is based on the mean function, robustness is often a concern to authors and data analysts. Specifically, the least squares algorithm provides a regression coefficient, $\hat{\beta}$, that minimizes the summed squared error:

$$\min_{\hat{\beta} \in R} \left[\sum_{i=1}^{n} (y_i - x_i \hat{\beta})^2 \right]. \tag{2.1}$$

So large deviations are made larger by squaring. The principle behind L-regression (also called quantile regression) is that a specific quantile, $\theta \in [0, 1]$, is selected and the following quantity is minimized:

$$\min_{\hat{\beta} \in R} \left[\sum_{i=1}^{n} \theta |y_i - x_i \hat{\beta}| + \sum_{i=1}^{n} (1 - \theta) |y_i - x_i \hat{\beta}| \right]. \tag{2.2}$$

Obviously, if $\theta = \frac{1}{2}$ the expression is greatly simplified and in fact becomes a well-known alternative to least squares estimates called the least absolute errors (LAE) estimator, the L_1 estimator, or the median regression estimator. Before the proliferation of statistical computing resources, calculating $\hat{\beta}$ coefficients was dramatically easier based on the objective in (2.1) than the objective in (2.2). However, the linear programming algorithm provided by Koenker and d'Orey (1993) provides quick solutions to the problem.

It has been shown by a number of authors that quantile regression estimates are more resistant to outliers (Koenker and Bassett 1978; Huber 1973, 1972; Tukey 1975), are asymptotically normal and in many cases are more efficient (smaller asymptotic variance) with wide-tailed distributions (Bassett and Koenker 1978; Buchinksy 1995), and can be thought of in wider context in terms of distribution of order statistics (Gutenbrunner and Jurečková 1992). Therefore in a number of data-analytic settings in which problematic distributions are masking desired measures of centrality, these tools can be very useful.

Unfortunately, there are some substantial difficulties with the use of quantile regression. The asymptotic precision of quantile regression coefficients (i.e., the asymptotic covariance matrix) depends on the inverse of a density function *evaluated at the specified quantile level* (Koenker 1994; Newey and Powell 1987); thus understanding the implications of the subsequent results is entirely dependent on empirically estimating this typically difficult function. In fact, the values of the test statistics depend substantively on the smoothing (Koenker and Bassett 1982; Wahba 1976) and resampling methods (Hahn 1995; Hall and Martin 1989) employed in this procedure. Also, the relative efficiency of quantile regression estimates depends not on the moments of the error structure, as one would expect, but instead on the precision of the chosen quantiles. This has two negative implications. First, except for large data sets, the discreteness of the quantiles implies that the choice of quantile will sharply affect the conclusions. Naturally, this effect is further worsened with clustered or skewed data. Second, if the distribution is reasonably normal, the quantile estimators will have little relative efficiency for typically chosen quantile levels. Regretfully, as is the case with several other theoretically complex statistical procedures, as popular commercial packages make calculations readily available and easy to perform, there are increased instances of applied work in which the researchers are not fully aware of these implications.

A broader theoretical issue in choosing SWAT versus quantile regression or any resistant technique is that the two approaches are fundamentally and philosophically completely different data treatments. As discussed at length in Chapter 1, SWAT seeks to find potentially important and prescriptive information contained in user-defined outlying cases. Conversely, robust regression techniques seek to minimize the impact of these *exact same cases* so as to get a more accurate picture of centrality in the dataset undisturbed (or less disturbed) by the mathematical inconvenience of summing large deviances. To say that these are diametrically opposed notions is hardly overstating the case. We believe that both robust/resistant techniques and SWAT belong on the practitioner's bookshelf and hope to illustrate situations where SWAT reveals previously difficult to obtain information from the data.

2.10 But So What?

Substantively weighted least squares is part of a general family of SWAT techniques; they can be used in many quantitative studies in public administration and public policy. SWAT is akin to sensitivity analysis in that it reveals what factors affect the best agencies or the best programs and put them into that elite category. The child support application described here is supplied as a practical example of the utility of SWAT techniques to public managers.

The SWAT process can be used to compare individual units within an organization, units in different organizations within the same jurisdiction (e.g., personnel offices), and organizations in different jurisdictions. If good performance measures exist, then SWAT will provide far more useful information than just regression alone. Both sets of results should be presented. The actual statistical process is relatively easy. Anyone with the skills to use regression can do SWLS, and the movement from SWLS to more advanced SWAT techniques is relatively direct.

SWAT is a methodology that can bridge the gap between academics and practitioners (see Chapter 1). Practitioners are interested in advice about what works best. That question is inherently different from the academic question of how something works. Regression deals with the academic question, but with some adjustments via SWAT it can also suggest what works best. SWAT is only the first step in this process. It identifies key variables that need to be examined in those programs that perform well. In this way it structures the process evaluation of the case studies; it does not say just look at program X to see why it is doing well, but look at program X and examine its Y processes. In this way SWAT avoids the pitfalls of the best practices approach.

The gap between academics and practitioners in public administration and public policy will not be completely closed. Many academics believe that they study public organizations to produce knowledge for its own sake rather than for any practical benefits. Such efforts provide valuable information to the profession even without obvious applications. We have outlined a methodology, SWAT, that is a bridge between academics and practitioners, is consistent with the reform traditions of public administration and public policy, and meets the scholarship standards of academic journals.

2.11 Addendum: Data Description

This section describes each of the variables and its source. The data and software to run the SWAT procedure are available at

http://people.tamu.edu/~kmeier.

Learning—Rate of change in child support collections per 1000 people in the population between 1982 and 1991. Source: Child Support Enforcement: Tenth, Thirteenth, and Sixteenth Annual Report to Congress.

Child Support Bureaucracy Expenditures—Average dollars of total administrative expenditures per 1000 people between 1982 and 1991. Source: Child Support Enforcement: Tenth, Thirteenth, and Sixteenth Annual Report to Congress.

Staff Increase—Staff in the child support bureaucracy in 1991 per million population minus staff in 1982 per million. Source: Child Support Enforcement: Tenth, Thirteenth, and Sixteenth Annual Report to Congress.

Slack Resources—Average of staff per caseload between 1982 and 1991. Source: Child Support Enforcement: Tenth, Thirteenth, and Sixteenth Annual Report to Congress.

Subject Ambiguity—Percentage of total caseload made up of non-AFDC cases. Source: Child Support Enforcement: Tenth, Thirteenth, and Sixteenth Annual Report to Congress.

Subject Instability—Standard deviation of the state bureaucracy's caseload, 1982 through 1991.

Demand—Percent divorced in each state, 1983–1991. Source: *Statistical Abstract of the United States*.

ACES Strength—Number of Association for Child Support Enforcement chapters per million in the population in 1991. Source: ACES.

Note: The different bases (1000 population versus 1 million) are used to scale the regression coefficients. They do not affect the actual results.

2.12 References

Alfasso, H., and J. Chakmakas. 1983. *Who Are We Missing? A Study of the Non-Paying Absent Parent in Albany.* New York: Bureau of Operations Analysis, Department of Social Services.

Andrews, David F. 1974. "A Robust Method for Multiple Linear Regression." *Technometrics* 16: 523–531.

Andrews, David F., P. J. Bickel, F. R. Hampel, P. J. Huber, W. H. Rogers, and John W. Tukey. 1972. *Robust Estimates of Location.* Princeton: Princeton University Press.

Barnett, Vic, and Toby Lewis. 1978. *Outliers in Statistical Data.* New York: Wiley.

Bartels, Larry. 1996. "Pooling Disparate Observations." *American Journal of Political Science* 40: 905–42.

Bassett, Gilbert, Jr., and Roger Koenker. 1978. "Asymptotic Theory of Least Absolute Regression." *Journal of the American Statistical Association* 73, 618–21.

Belsley, David A., Edwin Kuh, and Roy E. Welsch. 1980. *Regression Diagnostics.* New York: Wiley.

Birkes, David, and Yadolah Dodge. 1993. *Alternative Methods of Regression.* New York: Wiley.

Buchinsky, Moshe. 1995. "Estimating the Asymptotic Covariance Matrix for Quantile Regression Models. A Monte Carlo Study." *Journal of Econometrics* 68, 303–38.

Carroll, Raymond J., and David Ruppert. 1988. *Transforming and Weighting in Regression.* New York: Chapman & Hall.

Cook, Dennis R., and Sanford Weisberg. 1982. *Residuals and Influence in Regression.* New York: Chapman & Hall.

Edgeworth, F. V. 1883. "The Method of Least Squares." The London, Edinburgh, and Dublin Philosophical Magazine and Journal of Science, Series 5, 16: 360–75.

Emerson, J. D., and D. C. Hoaglin. 1983. "Resistant Lines for y Versus x." In *Understanding Robust and Exploratory Data Analysis*, edited by D. C. Hoaglin, Frederick Mosteller, and John Tukey. New York: Wiley.

2 An Introduction to Substantively Weighted Least Squares   *39*

Gill, Jeff. 1999. "The Insignificance of Null Hypothesis Significance Testing." *Political Research Quarterly* 52: 647–74.

Gutenbrunner, C., and J. Jurečková. 1992. "Regression Scores and Regression Quantiles." *Annals of Statistics* 20, 305–30.

Hahn, Jinyong. 1995. "Bootstrapping Quantile Regression Estimators." *Econometric Theory* 11, 105–21.

Hall, P., and M. A. Martin. 1989. "A Note on the Accuracy of Bootstrap Percentile Method Confidence Intervals for a Quantile." *Statistics and Probability Letters* 8, 197–200.

Hamilton, Lawrence C. 1992. *Regression with Graphics.* Pacific Grove, CA: Brooks/Cole.

Hampel, F. R. 1974. "The Influence Curve and its Role in Robust Estimation." *Journal of the American Statistical Association* 69, 383–93.

Hampel, F. R., E. M. Ronchetti, P. J. Rousseeuw, and W. A. Stahel. 1986. *Robust Statistics: The Approach Based on Influence Functions.* New York: Wiley.

Hoaglin, David C., Frederick Mosteller, and John W. Tukey. 1983. *Understanding Robust and Exploratory Data Analysis.* New York: Wiley.

Huber, P. J. 1981. *Robust Statistics.* New York: Wiley.

Huber, P. J. 1973. "Robust Regression: Asymptotics, Conjectures and Monte Carlo." *Annals of Statistics* 1, 799–821.

Huber, P. J. 1972. "Robust Statistics: A Review." *Annals of Mathematical Statistics* 43, 1041–67.

Keiser, Lael R. 1996. "Bureaucracy, Politics, and Public Policy: The Case of Child Support." Unpublished Ph.D. dissertation. University of Wisconsin-Milwaukee.

Klawitter, Marieka, and Irwin Garfinkel. 1991. "The Effects of Routine Income Withholding of Child Support on AFDC Participation and Costs." Discussion paper no. 961–91. Madison, Wisconsin: Institute for Research on Poverty.

Koenker, Roger. 1994. "Confidence Intervals for Regression Quantiles." *Asymptotic Statistics. Proceedings of the Fifth Prague Symposium,* 349–59.

Koenker, Roger, and Gilbert Bassett, Jr. 1982. "Robust Tests for Heteroscedasticity Based on Regression Quantiles." *Econometrica* 50: 43–61.

Koenker, Roger, and Gilbert Bassett, Jr. 1978. "Regression Quantiles." *Econometrica* 46, 33–50.

Koenker, Roger, and V. d'Orey. 1993. "A Remark on Computing Regression Quantiles." *Applied Statistics* 36, 383–93.

Krasker, W. S. 1980. "Estimation in Linear Regression Models with Disparate Data Points." *Econometrica* 48, 1333–46.

Kritzer, Herbert M. 1996. "The Data Puzzle: The Nature of Interpretation in Quantitative Research." *American Journal of Political Science* 40: 1–33.

Lebovic, James H. 1995. "How Organizations Learn: U.S. Government Estimates of Foreign Military Spending." *American Journal of Political Science* 39: 835–63.

Lynn, Lawrence E. 1987. "Public Management: 'What Do We Know? What Should We Know? and How Will We Know It?' " *Journal of Policy Analysis and Management* 7: 178–87.

Mazmanian, Daniel A., and Paul A. Sabatier. 1989. *Implementation and Public Policy.* Lanham, MD: University Press of America.

McDonald, J., and J. R. Moran. 1983. *Wisconsin Study of Absent Fathers: Ability to Pay Child Support.* Madison, WI: Wisconsin Department of Health and Social Services and Institute for Research on Poverty.

Michalopoulas, Charles, and Irwin Garfinkel. 1989. "Reducing Welfare Dependence and Poverty of Single Mothers by Means of Earnings and Child Support: Wishful Thinking and Realistic Possibilities." Discussion Paper no. 882–89. Madison, WI: Institute for Research on Poverty.

Newey, Whitney K., and James L. Powell. 1987. "Asymptotic Least Squares Estimation and Testing." *Econometrica* 55, 819–47.

Osborne, D., and T. Gaebler. 1992. *Reinventing Government.* Reading, MA: Addison-Wesley.

Overman, E. Sam, and Kathy J. Boyd. 1994. "Best Practice Research and Postbureaucratic Reform." *Journal of Public Administration Research and Theory* 4: 67–84.

Rousseeuw, Peter J., and Annick M. Leroy. 1987. *Robust Regression and Outlier Detection.* New York: Wiley.

Sabatier, Paul A., and Hank C. Jenkins-Smith. 1993. *Policy Change and Learning: An Advocacy Coalition Approach.* Boulder, CO: Westview Press.

Simon, Herbert A. 1969. *The Sciences of the Artificial.* Cambridge, MA: MIT Press.

Tukey, J. W. 1975. "Instead of Gauss–Markov Least Squares, What?" In *Applied Statistics*, edited by R. P. Gupta. Amsterdam: North Holland.

Wahba, Grace. 1976. "Histosplines with Knots Which Are Order Statistics." *Journal of the Royal Statistical Society* Series B 38, 140–51.

Weber, Max. 1946. *From Max Weber: Essays in Sociology.* H. H. Gerth and C. Wright Mills, trans. New York: Oxford University Press.

Western, Bruce. 1995. "Concepts and Suggestions for Robust Regression Analysis." *American Journal of Political Science* 39: 786–817.

Chapter 3

The Theory and Application of Generalized Substantively Reweighted Least Squares[1]

Jeff Gill, Kenneth J. Meier

3.1 Introduction

Linear modeling, regression in particular, has spawned more variations, more versions, and more enhancements than perhaps any other statistical procedure. A substantial amount of this literature focuses on robust and resistant techniques that compensate for undesirable properties in the data (Rousseeuw and Leroy 1987; Huber 1981; Hogg 1974; Andrews 1974). Substantively weighted analytical techniques (SWAT) come from a completely different perspective in which successful cases are treated as sources of important information. Whereas resistant techniques seek to minimize the effect of outliers, SWAT techniques specifically seek to analyze what makes the outliers distinguishable in terms of their use of resources. From a data-analytic standpoint, substantively weighted least squares (SWLS) seeks to identify a subset of the explanatory variables that most influence

---

[1]An earlier version of this chapter was prepared for delivery at 1998 Annual Meeting of the Western Political Science Association, Los Angeles, CA., March 19–21.

41

42   Jeff Gill, Kenneth J. Meier

successful programs. Unlike a more conventional approach to influence in regression (Chatterjee and Hadi 1988; Hampel 1974; Hampel et al. 1986; Rousseeuw and Leroy 1987), SWAT techniques do not see outliers as becoming potentially unbounded or even that they are necessarily undesirable elements of the data. This perspective sees outliers (on the positive side of the mean) as potential prescriptions for improving future performance.

In this chapter the SWLS procedure is generalized to apply to a wider range of applications. SWLS is based on simple multivariate linear regression. The SWLS procedure runs 10 consecutive weighted regression models on the same data (the first of which has uniform weighting equal to 1.0—i.e., unweighted standard linear (OLS) regression), consecutively downweighting by 0.10 each case whose externally Studentized (jackknifed) residual is less than 0.70. So after 10 iterations, high-performing cases will have weights at 1.0 and low performing cases will have weights at 0.1. At this point, variables whose regression coefficients are found to be different from OLS slopes are identified as indicating those factors that have a different effect on higher-performing cases. The model is intended to successfully identify the critical combination of inputs that cause particular state agencies to substantially increase their bureaucratic performance.

Why is this approach interesting? First consider the problem of defining high-performing cases without a specific methodology. Clearly, highly advantaged cases benefit from the corresponding levels of explanatory variables. Therefore it is difficult to assert that a high-performing case is doing well *given* a specific mix of inputs without looking at the corresponding residual. Conversely, a highly disadvantaged case may be performing extremely well relative to similarly affected cases but not relative to advantaged cases. In both scenarios, we are interested in residual outliers with all model-specified explanations included.

Why is this approach better than segmenting out high-performing cases and performing two analyses? The primary reason is that one needs to develop a model specification in order to get the residuals that determine high performance given relative benefits and hindrances. High performers are those cases that most exploit their available resources, not simply those with high values of the outcome variable. Second, it is possible, even likely, that segmenting out these cases sufficiently reduces the sample size that inference is difficult or unreliable. In the SWLS approach a focus is developed on the high-performing cases while the others are reduced in emphasis to a "background." In a sense we get the primary information about the coefficient effects on the high-performing cases where these results borrow strength from the full complement of cases.

The following section generalizes the SWLS procedure by using a series of transformations relating the jackknifed residuals to a common j-shaped tabular distribution. This extension, Generalized Substantively Reweighted Least Squares (GSRLS), allows us to develop alpha-level positive outlier identification applicable to a wide range of data-analytic settings. Furthermore, distributional determination

3 The Theory and Application of Generalized Substantively Reweighted Least Squares   *43*

of the threshold parameter (0.70 for SWLS) removes the arbitrariness of this selection.

3.2 Distribution of the Jackknifed Residuals

Suppose we have an ordinary least squares setup that meets the standard Gauss–Markov assumptions.[2] Define the terms conventionally:

$$\mathbf{Y} = \mathbf{X}\boldsymbol{\beta} + \boldsymbol{\varepsilon} \tag{3.1}$$

where $\mathbf{Y}$ is an $n \times 1$ vector of outcome variable values, $\mathbf{X}$ is an $n \times k$ and rank k matrix of explanatory variables with a leading vector of ones for the constant, $\boldsymbol{\beta}$ is a $k \times 1$ vector of coefficients to be estimated, and $\boldsymbol{\varepsilon}$ is a $n \times 1$ vector of errors. This model produces the following standard result for estimating $\hat{\mathbf{Y}}$:

$$\hat{\mathbf{Y}} = \mathbf{X}(\mathbf{X}'\mathbf{X})^{-1}\mathbf{X}'\mathbf{Y} = \mathbf{HY} \tag{3.2}$$

where $\mathbf{H}$ is the standard hat matrix, so named because $\mathbf{H}$ puts a hat on $\mathbf{Y}$ in equation (3.2). We define the model residuals, an $n \times 1$ vector, by

$$\mathbf{R} = \mathbf{Y} - \mathbf{HY} = (\mathbf{I} - \mathbf{H})\mathbf{Y} \tag{3.3}$$

where $\mathbf{I}$ is an $n \times n$ matrix with ones on the diagonal and zeros elsewhere (called the identity matrix and the multidimensional equivalent of the number 1). Thus under the Gauss–Markov assumptions:

$$E(\mathbf{R}) = \mathbf{0} \tag{3.4}$$

$$Var(\mathbf{R}) = (\mathbf{I} - \mathbf{H})\sigma^2 \tag{3.5}$$

$$Var(R_i) = (1 - h_{ii})\sigma^2 \tag{3.6}$$

where h_{ii} is the ith diagonal element of the hat matrix and R_i is the ith residual. Since σ^2 is unknown, use s^2 as the consistent estimate such that

$$s^2 = \frac{\mathbf{R}'\mathbf{R}}{n - k} \quad \text{and} \quad (s_i)^2 = (1 - h_{ii})s^2 \tag{3.7}$$

The ith jackknifed residual (also called an externally Studentized residual) is calculated from $s_{(i)}$, the estimate of σ when the regression is run omitting the ith case:

$$t_{(i)} = \frac{R_i}{s_{(i)}\sqrt{1 - h_{ii}}}. \tag{3.8}$$

---

[2]Very briefly, these assumptions are: (1) the functional form of the data is approximately linear, (2) the residuals are independent with expected value zero and constant variance, and (3) there is no correlation between any regressor and residual.

This statistic, $t_{(i)}$, can also be thought of as the residual weighted inversely proportional to the jackknifed standard error. One actually does not have to run n different regressions to obtain the vector of jackknifed standard errors; it can be calculated directly from

$$s_{(i)}^2 = \frac{(n-k)s^2 - \frac{R_i^2}{(1-h_{ii})}}{n-k-1}.$$

(3.9)

Now consider the statistic $d_{(i)}$, which is often used to create a likelihood ratio test of no outliers:

$$d_{(i)} = \frac{t_{(i)}^2}{n-k}.$$

(3.10)

Claim: $d_{(i)} \sim$ beta $(\frac{1}{2}, \frac{n-k-1}{2})$

Proof. We have $R_i \sim n(0, (1-h_{ii})\sigma^2)$ from the original regression assumptions. Thus

$$\frac{R_i}{\sqrt{1-h_{ii}}\sigma} \sim n(0, 1).$$

Therefore,

$$\left[\frac{R_i}{\sqrt{1-h_{ii}}\sigma}\right]^2 \sim \Gamma\left(\tfrac{1}{2}, 2\right)$$

(3.11)

where $\Gamma()$ denotes the gamma distribution and $\Gamma(\frac{1}{2}, 2)$ is an important special case: the chi-squared distribution with one degree of freedom. Using $n - k = \sum_{i=1}^{n}(1-h_{ii})$, $\mathbf{R'R} = (n-k)s^2$, and (3.9) yields

$$\sum_{i=1}^{n}\left[\frac{R_i}{\sqrt{1-h_{ii}}\sigma}\right]^2 = \frac{1}{\sigma^2}\sum_{i=1}^{n}\frac{R_i^2}{1-h_{ii}}$$

$$= \frac{1}{\sigma^2}\sum_{i=1}^{n}\left[s^2(n-k) - s_{(i)}^2(n-k-1)\right]$$

$$= \frac{1}{\sigma^2}\sum_{i=1}^{n}\left[\mathbf{R'R} - \mathbf{R'_{(i)}R_{(i)}}\right]$$

$$= \frac{1}{\sigma^2}\sum_{i=1}^{n}\left[R_i'R_i\right]$$

$$= (n-k)\frac{s^2}{\sigma^2}$$

(3.12)

where $(n-k)\frac{s^2}{\sigma^2}$ is well known to be distributed $\Gamma\left(\frac{n-k}{2}, 2\right)$. It follows from this result and the additive properties of independent variances and gamma distributed random variables that

$$\frac{s^2}{\sigma^2} = \frac{R_i^2}{(1-h_{ii})\sigma^2} + \frac{s_{(i)}^2}{\sigma^2}$$

so

$$(n-k)\frac{R_i^2}{(1-h_{ii})\sigma^2} \sim \Gamma(\tfrac{1}{2}, 2) \qquad \text{and} \qquad (n-k)\frac{s_{(i)}^2}{\sigma^2} \sim \Gamma\left(\frac{n-k-1}{2}, 2\right)$$

where each of the R_i is independently distributed from the ith jackknifed variance. So (3.10) can be rearranged in the following manner:

$$d_{(i)} = \frac{t_{(i)}^2}{n-k} = \frac{\frac{R_i^2}{(1-h_{ii})s_{(i)}^2}}{\frac{R_i}{(1-h_{ii})\sigma^2} + \frac{s_{(i)}^2}{\sigma^2}}. \tag{3.13}$$

Using (3.12) and independence of the two quantities, we have $d_{(i)} \sim \text{beta}\,(\tfrac{1}{2}, \frac{n-k-1}{2})$ by a standard transformation (Rohatgi 1976, p. 215; Casella and Berger 1990, p. 630). ∎

3.3 Relationship to the F Distribution

The utility of the claim presented and proven above is realized through the application of another well-known random variable transformation (Kennedy and Gentle 1980, p .219). Suppose

$$X \sim F(p, q).$$

Then

$$\frac{\frac{p}{q}X}{1 + \frac{p}{q}X} \sim \text{beta}\left(\frac{p}{2}, \frac{q}{2}\right).$$

Solving backward, we get the following useful transformation: If

$$X \sim \text{beta}\left(\frac{p}{2}, \frac{q}{2}\right)$$

then

$$\frac{\frac{q}{p}X}{1-X} \sim F(p, q).$$

So in the case of $d_{(i)} \sim \text{beta}(\frac{1}{2}, \frac{n-k-1}{2})$,

$$c_{(i)} = \frac{(n-k-1)d_{(i)}}{1-d_{(i)}} = \frac{n-k-1}{\frac{1}{d_{(i)}}-1} \sim F(1, n-k-1). \qquad (3.14)$$

This result is helpful because it allows us to use the common F distribution table with the first parameter equal to one. The nongeneralized SWLS procedure uses the value 0.7 as a threshold for dichotomizing high-performing agencies from the others. In the more generalized context, that would be equivalent to $\alpha = P(F > f)$ calculated as follows for the child support data ($n = 50, k = 7$):

$$c_{(i)} = \frac{n-k-1}{\frac{1}{d_{(i)}}-1} = \frac{50-7-1}{\frac{1}{\left(\frac{0.7^2}{50-7}\right)}-1} = 0.484121383.$$

Therefore selecting $t_{(i)} = 0.7$ produces $c_{(i)} = 0.484$ distributed $F_{1,42}$ for these data.

Even though the underlying probability density function (PDF) of the $c_{(i)}$ is continuous ($F_{1,n-k-1}$), the order statistics of the $c_{(i)}$, denoted $c_{((i))}$, are discrete and therefore have a probability mass function (PMF). From the theory of order statistics (Casella and Berger 1990; Stuart and Ord 1994), the probability that *exactly* r of the n values are less than some arbitrary value, γ, is

$$P[c_{((r \leq n))} \leq \gamma] = \binom{n}{r} [F(\gamma)]^r [1 - F(\gamma)]^{n-r} \qquad (3.15)$$

where $F(\gamma)$ denotes the cumulative distribution function (CDF) at some point γ. The CDF of the rth order statistic from the distribution of $c_{(i)}$ is given by

$$F_{c_{((i))}}(\gamma) = \sum_{j=r}^{n} \binom{n}{j} [F(\gamma)]^j [1 - F(\gamma)]^{n-j} \qquad (3.16)$$

which is the probability that at least r observations are not greater than γ: $x_{(r)} \leq \gamma$ (the probability that r or more of the order statistics are less than the selected threshold). If we continue with the running example of the child support data in Chapter 2, $F_{45}(0.484) \approx 0$, $F_{30}(0.484) = 0.127$, and $F_{25}(0.484) = 0.609$. This probability increases as r decreases since it becomes easier to claim this number of values below the threshold.

Out of fifty states, SWLS finds that seven child support programs meet the criterion of high performance. The probability that at least 43 observations are lower than 0.484 is almost zero, which is also the probability that at most 7 observations are greater than 0.484. However, we are really interested in the probability that at least 7 observations are *above* the threshold, which is the probability that at most 43 observations are less than the threshold. By this way of thinking, the analyst can gauge the probability that an arbitrary subset will be

3 The Theory and Application of Generalized Substantively Reweighted Least Squares 47

in the select, unweighted group after the SWAT procedure. This probability is given by

$$P[c_{((n-r))} > \gamma] = \sum_{j=1}^{r-1} \binom{n}{j} [F(\gamma)]^j [1 - F(\gamma)]^{n-j}. \qquad (3.17)$$

From our example, $P[c_{((7))} > 0.484] = 0.99$, meaning that we are almost guaranteed to get the desired (actually observed) 7 values in the select group. Suppose we wanted to know the probability that half of the states end up in the unweighted category. This is simply $P[c_{((25))} > 0.484] = 0.39$. More important, the analyst can adjust the threshold to obtain a desired inclusion probability. Suppose it was desired a priori that 5 cases be considered as high-performing and therefore unweighted. What would be a reasonable threshold for the jackknifed residual that provides a high probability of including at least 5 cases? From (3.17), $P[c_{((5))} > 1.5] = 0.98$, and backing $c_{(i)} = 1.5$ through (3.14) and (3.10) produces a jackknifed residual threshold of

$$t_{(i)} = \sqrt{\frac{(n-k)c_{(i)}}{c_{(i)} + n - k - 1}} = 1.218 \qquad (3.18)$$

where absolute valuation inside the radical is not necessary because the term can never be negative. So the policy analyst has great flexibility with the SWAT construction in that the definition of high performance as a ratio of the total number of cases can be determined probabilistically from the distribution of the transformed jackknifed residuals. Conversely, the procedure can be performed with conventional parameters (SWLS), and the subsequent probabilities can be calculated, allowing great flexibility both in exploratory data analysis and reporting criteria. The first generalization from SWLS to GSRLS is then the ability to alter the threshold according to a desired size of the outlying group.

3.4 Five Assumptions and a Warning

Classic linear regression models require five general assumptions (Amemiya 1985; Greene 1999). It is clearly important to discuss SWLS and GSRLS in the context of these standard requirements. Suppose that the final GSRLS weights are expressed as the diagonal matrix $\mathbf{D}^{-\frac{1}{2}}$, where the inverse square root is used purely for compatibility to common weighting notation in linear models. Then the GSRLS model is expressed as

$$\mathbf{D}^{-\frac{1}{2}}\mathbf{Y} = \mathbf{D}^{-\frac{1}{2}}\mathbf{X}\boldsymbol{\beta} + \mathbf{D}^{-\frac{1}{2}}\boldsymbol{\varepsilon}$$
$$\mathbf{Y}^* = \mathbf{X}^*\boldsymbol{\beta} + \boldsymbol{\varepsilon}^*.$$

Thus the GSRLS result fits the linear model functional form. The second requirement is that the disturbance term have zero mean:

$$E(\varepsilon^*) = E(\mathbf{D}^{-\frac{1}{2}}\varepsilon) = \mathbf{D}^{-\frac{1}{2}}E(\varepsilon) = \mathbf{0}.$$

We next consider the variance term, which does not produce such clean results:

$$Var(\varepsilon^*) = Var(\mathbf{D}^{-\frac{1}{2}}\varepsilon) = \mathbf{D}^{-\frac{1}{2}}Var(\varepsilon)\mathbf{D}^{-\frac{1}{2}} = \sigma^2\mathbf{D}^{-1}.$$

There are two implications. First, since there are no off-diagonal elements in $\sigma^2\mathbf{D}^{-1}$, the required assumption of no autocorrelation is met. Second, since the diagonal values are necessarily different, the GSRLS result is not guaranteed to meet the homoscedasticity requirement. For this reason, it is essential that the distribution of the residuals be tested or visually inspected in the final model. There is a plethora of tests for heteroscedasticity in linear models (including White, Breusch–Pagan, Goldfeld–Quandt, and Glesjer's), and several graphical approaches such as residual dependence plots and normal-quantile plots. The examples developed here use both of these visual approaches to looking for this possibly introduced heteroscedasticity. The final standard assumption requires that there be no correlation between regressor and disturbance:

$$Cov(x_i^*, \varepsilon_i^*) = Cov(d_{ii}^{-\frac{1}{2}}x_i, d_{ii}^{-\frac{1}{2}}\varepsilon_i) = d_{ii}^{-1}Cov(x_i, \varepsilon_i) = 0.$$

Thus the single caution, and not a minor one, is that the practitioner should ensure that the GSRLS process does not introduce heteroscedastic effects through the iterative weighting process. However, this caution is restricted to the interpretation of SWAT results as linear model coefficients and estimates of population parameters. Since we are *not* interested in identifying unknown population centralities, this is not an important problem. Our interest lies instead on a select group of cases that contain prescriptive information.

3.5 Using the GSRLS Procedure

One obvious issue with the SWLS procedure is the arbitrariness of the jackknifed residuals threshold parameter (0.7) and the number of downweighting iterations (10). The GSRLS procedure addresses this issue by allowing any α-level threshold test based on the F distribution of the statistic in (3.14). Furthermore, the number of downweighting iterations, and therefore the size of the downweights, is easily manipulated. Suppose we define a new parameter, β, which represents the number of downweighting cycles starting at 1 (the first nonweighted least squares regression). Therefore each weight is decreased by $\frac{1}{\beta}$ for cases whose statistic does not exceed the critical value from the F distribution determined by the chosen α. For SWLS this β is fixed at 10, so the decrement and the stopping point are fixed at

3 The Theory and Application of Generalized Substantively Reweighted Least Squares   49

$\frac{1}{10}$. Recall also that SWLS does not reweight after each iteration in the procedure. With GSRLS the investigator can define any desired size for β. The chapter addendum contains an Splus/R implementation of the GSRLS procedure that allows user determination of α and β.

So what values for α and β lead to meaningful analyses? Figure 3.1 shows slope changes against the range of α for the seven variables in the child support

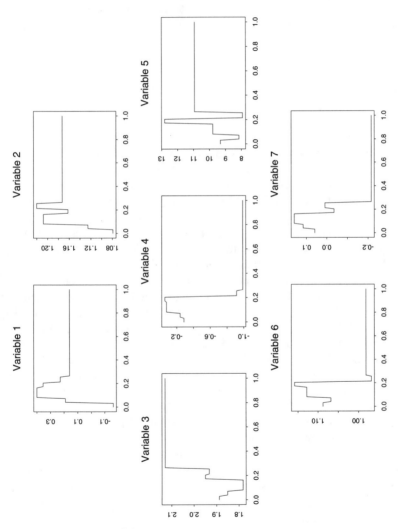

Figure 3.1 Slope Changes by α, Child Support Data

data from Chapter 2. The slope values converge at about $\alpha = 0.3$ for all seven variables, requiring a jackknifed residual threshold of 0.1475 (from 3.18). So in the case of this data set, we could have been even less strict than the seemingly generous $\alpha = \int_0^{0.484} f_F(x)dx = 0.5096$. One basic approach is to perform this exact process to determine slope changes for values over the range of α. This is clearly analogous to determining p-values for the threshold of convergence of the slope changes. Note, however, that the interpretation is different in the sense that these are not significance levels in the traditional Fisherian sense. A similar analysis with regard to differing levels of β shows that this parameter is much less important in determining high-performance-affecting explanatory variables. Generally β values greater than 20 are not required.

3.6 A Simple Example

This section presents a simple example from a deliberately small sample using data from an 1854 study on mental health in the fourteen counties of Massachusetts. The study was conducted by Edward Jarvis, who was then president of the American Statistical Association, and is discussed more recently by Hunter (1987). In the vernacular of the time, Dr. Jarvis investigated (without using a linear model) the number of lunatics per county and the tendency to care for them at home. The explanatory variables are number of lunatics per county (NBR), distance to the nearest mental healthcare center (DIST), population in the county by thousands (POP), population per square county mile (PDEN). The outcome variable is the percent of lunatics cared for in the home (PHOME).

It is often the case that the quality of the model fit can be improved substantially by transforming the variables. Pathologies that call for some mathematical transformation on some variable include strong skewness in either direction, large outliers, and clustering or batching. Also, for the linear model and extensions to the linear model, it is sometimes the case that the linearity of the relationship between explanatory variables and the outcome variable (i.e., the first Gauss–Markov assumption) can be improved by transformations. Typical approaches include power and root transformations, inverses, logarithms, and exponentiation. Although there is no set rule as to the extent of complexity of the transformation (provided it is invariant to order), more intricate approaches often lead to model results that are difficult or impossible to interpret.

Figure 3.2 displays a scatterplot matrix of each of the variables against the others with a nonparametric cubic smoothing spline overlaid. A smoothing spline is simply a trace of the trend of the data that maximizes closeness to the data subject to a numerical penalty for being overly "wiggly."[3] This is a useful tool in

---

[3] See Hastie and Tibshirani 1990, Chapter 2, for a detailed discussion of this and other smoothers.

3 The Theory and Application of Generalized Substantively Reweighted Least Squares 51

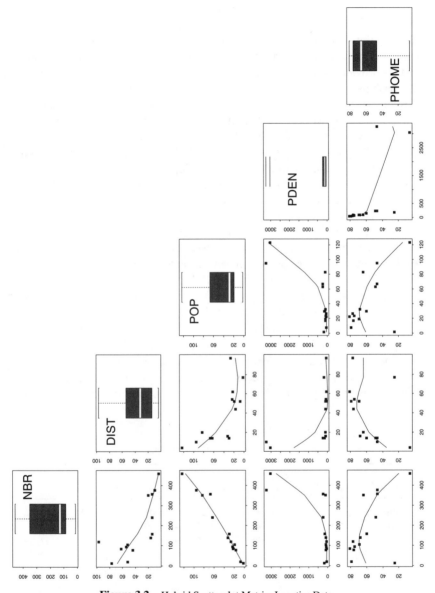

Figure 3.2 Hybrid Scatterplot Matrix, Lunatics Data

52   *Jeff Gill, Kenneth J. Meier*

that it assists the eye in seeing nonlinear trends in the scatterplots. The diagonal cells also provide a univariate boxplot of the listed variable corresponding to that row and column in the figure. Boxplots portray the interquartile range (middle 50%) of the data as the length of the box, with the median given by the inner line, and the points 1.5 times the interquartile range in both directions indicated by the outer "fences." Points outside the fences are indicated by straight lines. Figure 3.2 thus provides both a univariate distributional measure, but also a sense of the relationships between variables, the most important of which are the relationships between the explanatory variables and the outcome variable. This exploratory data analysis tool not only helps to determine whether transformations are warranted, but also provides suggestions as to the form.

The scatterplots indicate that POP and PDEN have some right-hand-side skewness (particularly PDEN). Correspondingly, a log transformation is applied in both cases. An inverse transformation on DIST is applied, and NBR is left in its original state. It should be noted that many different transformations can be applied to any single variable and that there is no one "correct answer." These transformations are selected for simplicity and because they do provide a better model. The interested reader is strongly encouraged to obtain the data from the authors' Web site and develop better fits to the data as a means of understanding transformations. The subsequent OLS model is provided in Table 3.1. Except for the variable for the log of population density, each of these variables appears to be a strong explanatory factor (95% confidence intervals bounded away from zero). Table 3.2 shows the SWLS analysis for these same data ($\beta = 10$, $\alpha = 0.7$, so $c_{(i)} = 0.46$).

Figure 3.3 shows the internally Studentized residuals ($R_i/(s\sqrt{1 - h_{ii}})$) as vertical lines and externally Studentized or jackknifed residuals ($R_i/(s_{(i)}\sqrt{1 - h_{ii}})$) as points. This diagnostic can be used to check the influence of individual data points as measured by the residual difference from jackknifing out. Note that there

Table 3.1   Ordinary Least Squares Model, Lunatics Data

Outcome Variable = Percent Cared for in the Home				
Explanatory Variable	Coefficient	Std Error	t-stat	95% CI
Intercept	39.511	19.726	2.003	[0.848: 78.174]
NBR	−0.146	0.047	−3.099	[−0.238: −0.054]
inv(DIST)	−189.396	70.349	−2.692	[−327.280:−51.512]
log(POP)	21.587	4.562	4.732	[12.645: 30.529]
log(PDEN)	−2.965	3.430	−0.864	[−9.688: 3.758]

Adjusted $R^2 = 0.91$

$F = 22.82396$ on 4 and 9 degrees of freedom

Residual Standard Error = 7.93 on 9 degrees of freedom

3 The Theory and Application of Generalized Substantively Reweighted Least Squares

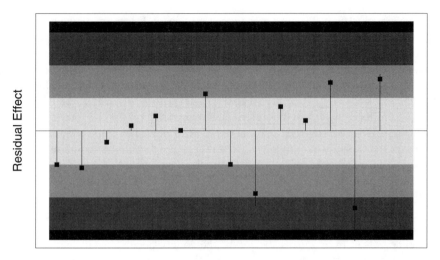

Figure 3.3 Residual Diagnostic Plot: Lunatics Data

is only one case (Nantucket because of its great geographical isolation) where there is a great discrepancy.

Looking at the SWLS results in Table 3.2, we can conclude that the counties that were "more successful" (i.e., provided more home care, if that is desirable) were more affected by the inverse distance variable. This observation certainly agrees with common sense: they were probably doing so out of necessity. Interestingly, the number of lunatics per county variable is less important to these counties

Table 3.2 SWLS Model, Lunatics Data

Explanatory Variable	Coefficient	Std Error	t-stat	95% CI	
Intercept	48.847	15.446	3.162	[18.573:	79.121]
NBR	−0.143	0.051	−2.804	[−0.243:	−0.043]
inv(DIST)	−214.363	40.204	−5.332	[−293.163:	−135.563]
log(POP)	18.968	6.330	2.997	[6.561:	31.375]
log(PDEN)	−1.832	1.878	−0.976	[−5.513:	1.849]

Outcome Variable = Percent Cared for in the Home

Adjusted $R^2 = 0.96$
$F = 51.06451$ on 4 and 9 degrees of freedom
Residual Standard Error = 3.99 on 9 degrees of freedom

54   Jeff Gill, Kenneth J. Meier

than the typical case as represented in the OLS model. Furthermore, the log of the population density has a 95% confidence interval bounding zero. Thus the interrelated variables of number of cases and the population from which they are drawn change when we use SWLS to isolate the positive-side outliers. The probability of obtaining these four cases as unweighted, "high performers" is calculated as $P[c_{(11)} > 0.46] = \sum_{j=1}^{10} \binom{14}{j} [F(0.46)]^j [1 - F(0.46)]^{14-j} = 0.929$.

The GSRLS analysis of these same data is provided in Table 3.3 for the purpose of comparison. We stated earlier that the GSRLS procedure imposes greater hurdles for the isolation of outlying cases; it is apparent that this increased selectivity changes the results. Suppose that we want the final number of unweighted cases also to be two, thus being more selective than SWLS. If we select $c_{(i)} = 2$, then $P[c_{(11)} > 2.0] = 0.789$.

The picture is quite different given the reweighting combined with $\beta = 50$ and $\alpha = 2$. Now the only explanatory variable with a 95% confidence interval bounded away from zero is the log of the county population. In fact, the two cases that remain isolated are those with the largest population values (Essex and Suffolk). It is curious that the counties that include the largest cities, and presumably ready access to mental healthcare facilities, are more affected by the population density in a way that inclines lunatics to receive care in the home.

The primary point here is that one gets a different picture with each of these three analytical approaches. With the OLS model, we understand how typical cases are affected and can apply standard inferential methods from linear model theory. With the SWLS model, we get an interesting picture of a reasonably differentiated group of counties, which provides new insights with regard to two of the factors. Continuing with the selectivity process, by setting the parameters in a highly selective fashion (not available with SWLS), we can further raise the requirements and thereby get an even smaller group of positive-side outliers. This

Table 3.3   GSRLS Model, Lunatics Data

Explanatory Variable	Outcome Variable = Percent Cared for in the Home			
	Coefficient	Std Error	t-stat	95% CI
Intercept	45.835	22.110	2.073	[2.499: 89.171]
NBR	−0.180	0.081	−2.205	[−0.339:−0.021]
inv(DIST)	−187.264	96.253	−1.946	[−375.920: 1.392]
log(POP)	19.187	7.552	2.541	[4.385: 33.989]
log(PDEN)	−0.018	3.318	−0.005	[−6.521: 6.485]

Adjusted $R^2 = 0.94$
$F = 37.62251$ on 4 and 9 degrees of freedom
Residual Standard Error = 1.99 on 9 degrees of freedom
Unweighted Cases: First Iteration = 4, Last Iteration = 2

3 The Theory and Application of Generalized Substantively Reweighted Least Squares   *55*

last analysis leads to the conclusion that in these isolated cases, one factor in particular (which did not stand out before) is seen to be more important.

3.7 SWAT Versus the Chow Test

A common technique in applied econometrics is to segment a dataset into two possibly dissimilar groups, run the standard linear model on each group and the pooled group, and then use the results to build a test statistic to test the hypothesis of a difference between the two groups. The process works as follows. Suppose we have a dataset of size N in which we would like to test whether there is a statistical difference between n and m of the cases, where $n + m = N$, given that all of the assumptions of the linear model hold. If we apply OLS we can easily get the following three quantities, which are, respectively, the residual sum of squares for the model for the first n cases, the model for the m additional cases that might or might not be logically grouped with the first n, and the pooled model where they are treated as indistinct (i.e., they are restricted to producing the same coefficient estimate, $\beta_n = \beta_m$):

$$SS_n = \sum_{i=1}^{n} R_i^2 \qquad SS_m = \sum_{i=n+1}^{N} R_i^2 \qquad SS_N = \sum_{i=1}^{N} R_i^2 .$$

From these quantities we can build a test statistic:

$$f = \frac{(SS_N - SS_n - SS_m)/k}{(SS_n + SS_m)/(n + m - 2k)}$$

where k is the number of coefficients including the constant. As the notation suggests, this test statistic is distributed according to the F distribution, with k and $n + m - 2k$ degrees of freedom (Chow 1960, p. 604). Obtaining a test statistic in the tail of the F distribution for some given α level is considered evidence to reject the null hypothesis of no difference between the groups.

It is clear that this test can actually be related to the underlying theory of SWAT since they are both built upon the linear model and an F test from the analysis of variance. Why might we prefer the use of one over another? The Chow test is particularly handy when the criterion suggesting segmentation into the two groups is very clear. Examples in the literature include motivations behind purchasing new cars versus used cars (Chow 1960), employment levels during war and non-war years (Greene 1999), and differences in pricing decisions by firms across specific geographic areas (Greenhut et al. 1980). However, when the segmentation criterion is not so easily hypothesized, then a much more arbitrary categorization is required. Furthermore, this may not be an easy distinction even to imagine. Take the (relevant) case of bureaucratic performance given levels of available resources. Segmentation is not even possible until an initial model is run and then it may not be easy to decide on a criterion statistic or threshold value.

More theoretically important, the Chow test gives a result that is based on predefinition of the two groups. A major advantage of SWAT techniques is that they evaluate the influence of cases individually through the magnitude of the jackknifed residual. Therefore, collinear effects that might otherwise drive the results seen in the Chow F test cannot affect the decision to place a case into the selected group. Once SWAT has selected the subgroup (high performers, failures, etc.), then the researcher can employ the Chow test if desired, except that a decision to make the segmentation and evaluate the groups separately means that the subgroup of interest is not evaluated with the entire sample as background. This limitation can range from a trivial issue (large samples, sharp differences), to major problems (very small subgroups, nearly identical behavior).

In short, we believe that the Chow test is very useful for large sample sizes and situations where the potential cleavage is clearly defined. In other cases, clearly the numerically greater class, SWAT will likely be much more valuable to the researcher. A final admonition is warranted as well. The Chow test leads naturally to null hypothesis significance testing of the flawed variety employed in the social sciences. We urge the practitioner to avoid that practice here.

3.8 Discussion

A central point is that the GSRLS procedure can be used to isolate particular mixtures of explanatory effects without an arbitrary and difficult segregation. A particular case-type is identified and the mixture of explanatory effects is developed borrowing strength from the full sample without fully diluting the case-specific information desired. An important and useful application lies in prescriptive analysis and therefore public management situations.

The GSRLS procedure suggests several extensions. For instance, Cook and Weisberg (1982, pp .191–9) propose a form of the Studentized residual particularly suited to generalized linear models that incorporates the link function. For simple logistic regression, theirs is a modified score test statistic for the null hypothesis where the expected information matrix is replaced by the observed information matrix. Chatterjee and Hadi (1988) look at models where the effects of simultaneously jackknifing observations *and* variables are investigated using a partial F-test. Their work relates to the GSRLS procedure in that simultaneous omission of the ith observation and the jth variable can illuminate influence factors that result from interrelationships between these variables and observations; this is exactly what GSRLS does except only with regard to influences on high-performing cases. A Bayesian approach could be developed whereby the initial threshold settings are treated as priors and updated throughout the iterations. This

3 The Theory and Application of Generalized Substantively Reweighted Least Squares **57**

approach, though considerably more computer-intensive, has the potential to reduce the burden of α level determination. In general, GSRLS can be seen as a
data-analytic tool that exploits certain characteristics of the linear model to find
a variable's influence on "successful" cases. As a result, many of the extensions
and variations of the linear model are likely to apply.

3.9 Addendum: Splus/R Code for SWAT

```
# This function uses qr decomposition with jackknifing to get
# the externalized residuals.
gsrls.t <- function(in.mat,W)  {
   X <- sqrt(W)%*%(cbind(Intercept=1,in.mat[,1:ncol(in.mat)-1]))
   Y <- s.i.jack <- t.i.jack <- as.vector(sqrt(W)%*%in.mat[,ncol(in.mat)])
   H <- hat(X)
   R <- qr.resid(qr(X),Y)
   for(i in 1:nrow(in.mat))  {
      R.jack <- qr.resid(qr(X[-i,]),Y[-i])
      s.i.jack[i] <- sqrt( (1-H[i])*(t(R.jack)%*%R.jack)/(nrow(X)-1-ncol(X)-1) )
      t.i.jack[i] <- R[i]/(s.i.jack[i]*sqrt(1-H[i]))
   }
   return(t.i.jack)
}
# this function returns the regression coefficients given a data
# matrix and weights
gsrls.l <- function(in.mat,W)  {
   X <- in.mat[,1:ncol(in.mat)-1]
   Y <- in.mat[,ncol(in.mat)]
   lm.out <- lm(Y ~ X, weights=diag(W))
   return( summary(lm.out)$coefficients,RSQ=summary(lm.out)$r.squared,
      F=summary(lm.out)$fstatistic, Std.Err=summary(lm.out)$sigma )
}
# This is the main function for gsrls, Input is an arbitrary size matrix: [X|Y],
# alpha, beta, and an operations flag.  Operations flag: 1 for optimizing, 2 for
# failure, 3 for risk averse.  Reweight=1 means GSRLS, anything else means SWLS
gsrls3 <- function (in.mat, alpha = 0.484124, beta = 10, op.flag = 1, reweight = 1)
{
               W <- diag(nrow(in.mat))
               initial.results <- gsrls.l(in.mat, W)
               threshold <- sqrt((alpha * (nrow(in.mat) - ncol(in.mat) - 1))/
                  (nrow(in.mat) - ncol(in.mat) - 2 + alpha))
               for (i in 1:(beta - 1))  {
                  if ((reweight == 1) || (i == 1)) jack.resid <- gsrls.t(in.mat, W)
                  w <- rep(1, nrow(W))
                  if (op.flag == 1) w[jack.resid <  threshold] <- 1 - i * (1/beta)
                  if (op.flag == 2) w[jack.resid > -threshold] <- 1 - i * (1/beta)
                  if (op.flag == 3) w[jack.resid < -threshold] <- 1 - i * (1/beta)
                  diag(W) <- w
                  if (i == 1) start.unweighted <- sum(w[w == 1])
               }
               end.unweighted <- sum(w[w == 1])
               list(gsrls.l(in.mat, W), start.unweighted = start.unweighted,
                     end.unweighted = end.unweighted, W = diag(W))
}
```

3.10 References

Amemiya, Takeshi. 1985. *Advanced Econometrics*. Cambridge, MA: Harvard University Press.

Andrews, D. F. 1974. "A Robust Method for Multiple Linear Regression." *Technometrics* 16: 523–31.

Casella, George, and Roger L. Berger. 1990. *Statistical Inference*. Pacific Grove, CA: Wadsworth & Brooks/Cole.

Chatterjee, Samprit, and Ali S. Hadi. 1988. *Sensitivity Analysis in Linear Regression* New York: Wiley.

Chow, Gregory C. 1960. "Tests of Equality Between Sets of Coefficients in Two Linear Regressions." *Econometrica* 28: 591–604.

Cook, Dennis R., and Sanford Weisberg. 1982. *Residuals and Influence in Regression* New York: Chapman & Hall.

Greene, William. 1999. *Econometric Analysis*. Fourth edition. New York: Macmillan.

Greenhut, John, M. L. Greenhut, and Sheng-Yung Li. 1980. "Spatial Pricing Patterns in the United States." *The Quarterly Journal of Economics* 94: 329–50.

Hampel, Frank R. 1974. "The Influence Curve and Its Role in Robust Estimation." *Journal of the American Statistical Association* 62: 1179–86.

Hampel, Frank, Elvezio M. Ronchetti, Peter J. Rousseeuw, and Werner A. Stahl. 1986. *Robust Statistics: The Approach Based on Influence Functions*. New York: Wiley.

Hastie, T. J., and R. J. Tibshirani. 1990. *Generalized Additive Models*. New York: Chapman & Hall.

Hogg, R. V. 1974. "Adaptive Robust Procedures: A Partial Review and Some Suggestions for Future Applications and Theory." *Journal of the American Statistical Association* 69: 909–23.

Huber, P. 1981. *Robust Statistics*. New York: Wiley.

Hunter, J. M. 1987. "Need and Demand for Mental Health Care: Massachusetts 1854." *The Geographic Review* 77: 139–156.

Kennedy, William J., and James E. Gentle. 1980. *Statistical Computing*. New York: Marcel Dekker.

Rohatgi, V. K. 1976. *An Introduction to Probability Theory and Mathematical Statistics*. New York: Wiley.

Rousseeuw, Peter J., and Annick M. Leroy. 1987. *Robust Regression and Outlier Detection*. New York: Wiley.

Stuart, Alan, and J. Keith Ord. 1994. *Kendall's Advanced Theory of Statistics*. New York: Edward Arnold.

Chapter 4
Substantively Weighted Analytical Techniques for Successes and Failures: SWLS and GSRLS[1]

Jeff Gill, Kenneth J. Meier

4.1 Introduction

The research literature on bureaucracy generally assumes that bureaucrats are risk averse, and some work goes further to characterize bureaucrats as risk avoiding and conservative (LaPiere 1965; Sjoberg, Brymer, and Farris 1966; Wolman 1971; Boyer 1973; Kaufman 1981). At the same time, the prescriptive literature, the most recent being the reinventing government movement (Osborne and Gaebler 1992; see also Barzelay 1992; Johnston 1993; Report of the National Performance Review, 1993), requires bureaucrats to be entrepreneurs, individuals who take major risks in an effort to achieve major performance breakthroughs. Although diametrically opposed in terms of objectives (scholarship versus practical advice),

---

[1]An earlier version of this chapter was given at the Fourth National Public Management Research Conference, Atlanta, Georgia, October 30–November 1, 1997. All data and documentation to replicate this work can be found at `http://people.tamu.edu/~kmeier`.

59

60   *Jeff Gill, Kenneth J. Meier*

both stress a concern with individuals and agencies that deviate from the norm (those that fail and those that succeed beyond expectations).

In situations such as these, we argue that traditional regression methods serve public administration and thus public management poorly (see Chapter 2). Regression-based techniques seek to generalize to the average case, a situation that neither the performance-optimizing nor the risk-averse literature sees as crucial. Perhaps the most critical comment in regard to the methodological development of public administration is our contention that as scholars of public management become better schooled in the more advanced techniques of regression, they will be progressing down the wrong road.

This chapter continues the explanation of substantively weighted analytical techniques (SWAT) using a dataset of 534 school districts in Texas. Specifically, it contrasts the differences among risk-averse bureaucracies, failing bureaucracies, and performance-optimizing bureaucracies. The intuition behind SWAT is that not all public management cases are of equal interest to either scholars or practitioners. Practitioners might be interested in agencies that perform better than average given the constraints the agency faces (e.g., the best-performing urban school district) or in agencies that avoid failure in the face of complex tasks and uncooperative environments (avoiding bank failures, space stations that fall apart; see Romzek and Dubnick, 1987, and Heimann, 1993 on the *Challenger* disaster). The way to incorporate these practitioner concerns into academic research is to focus on the residuals from a regression that has agency performance as outcome variable and agency inputs and policies as the explanatory variables. In Chapter 2 we were interested only in optimal performance so we suggested dealing with those cases whose external Studentized residuals were greater than 0.7. Rather than downweighting these extreme cases as a traditional regression analysis might do, we suggested that these cases should be overweighted (or the other cases downweighted) to determine how optimally performing agencies differ from the average agency. We downweighted the average agencies in a series of regressions by increments of 0.1 until the average cases were counted as equal to only 0.1 high-performing case. The changes found in these regressions, we contend, indicate the unique management elements that distinguish an excellent agency from a mediocre one.

From a statistical point of view, SWAT assumes that the regression coefficients vary across agencies. One of the differences between an excellent agency and a poor agency is that the excellent one gets far more output for a given level of input. That difference will show up in the weighted regressions when compared to the ordinary least squares regressions.

Meier and Keiser (1996) contended that substantively weighted least squares (SWLS) was general enough to deal with most values that concern public administration, although their analysis dealt only with optimal performance. Meier, Wrinkle, and Polinard (1999) took the approach one step further and looked at

4 Substantively Weighted Analytical Techniques for Successes and Failures: SWLS & GSRLS

agency performance but added the constraint that the performance must be equitable on racial grounds. The current chapter takes a third step by dealing with both the successes and the failures of public management.

4.2 The Dataset

The only restriction on the application of SWAT is that one needs measures of agency performance.[2] Our dataset is 534 Texas school districts, which is essentially the universe of Texas school districts with more than 500 students and at least 10 percent minority population. All data were gathered by the Texas Education Agency and are for the 1990–91 school year.

4.2.1 The Outcome Variable

Students in all Texas school districts at the time had to take a standardized achievement test in the third, fifth, seventh, ninth, and eleventh grades, thus creating uniform measures of student achievement and district performance.[3] Our outcome variable is the percentage of students in each district who passed this exam; the mean for all districts was 55.9.

4.2.2 The Explanatory Variables

Resources and policies are traditionally linked to educational performance with an education production function (Burtless 1996).[4] School district performance should be a function of environmental constraints, resources applied to the process, and district policies designed to improve performance. All performance models of public bureaucracy need to control for the type of inputs the bureaucracy receives. In the context of educational policy, poverty is a serious constraint on the educational performance of students. Poverty not only means students do not have access to learning tools in the home (computers, pre-K programs, etc.), but also it is often correlated with a less stable and less supportive home environment (e.g., single-parent households, high rates of teen pregnancy, and

---

[2]This is not actually a statistical restriction but a substantive one. The technique can be used in any regression; what makes the technique useful to public management is that it is used on performance models.

[3]Student test scores are not the only possible measure of organizational performance in education. Graduation rates, skills imparted, successful employment, or placement in higher education are other possible output indicators. Because much of the policy literature and the policy debate focuses on standardized test scores, we are comfortable using this measure.

[4]This literature is far too large to cite comprehensively. See the extended bibliography in Burtless (1996).

62   *Jeff Gill, Kenneth J. Meier*

low educational expectations; Necochea and Cune 1996; Fuller et al. 1996). Our measure of poverty is the percentage of students from low-income families.[5] The relationship to performance should be negative.

Poverty is, of course, highly correlated with race and ethnicity. The performance of minority students has been an especially prominent concern in some research (Fernandez and Velez 1985; Kickbusch 1985; Moore and Smith 1986; Meier and Stewart 1991; Rong and Grant 1992). As a result of a combination of prior discrimination, family instability, and lack of exposure to other developmental resources, minority students often pose serious challenges to a school district. This study will include the percentage of black and the percentage of Latino students as additional measures of educational constraints.

The relationship between expenditures and educational outcomes is one of the most contested relationships in educational policy. Examining a wealth of studies, Hanushek (1996, 1989, 1986) contends that there is no consistent relationship between money and student outcomes. Although this finding has been challenged by others (Hedges and Greenwald 1996), it remains the conventional wisdom. Economists, and Hanushek in particular (1994, 1986, 1981), perceive very small or zero marginal returns for increased spending. This argument emphasizes the alternate *use* of money rather than just a blind increase in appropriations (Coleman 1986; Mann and Inman 1984; Rossmiller 1987; Walberg and Fowler 1987). On the other side are education scholars such as Hedges et al. (1996, 1994) who find strong empirical links between per-pupil expenditures and learning outcomes. In recent longitudinal studies, however, money does appear to matter. Murray (1995) and Murray, Evans, and Schwab (1995) found that districts that increased expenditures had improved performance afterward. Smith and Meier (1994) showed that expenditures should be considered long-term investments that influence performance only after a time lag.

Three expenditure variables are included in the analysis: per-pupil expenditures for instruction, the average teacher salary, and the percentage of money from state funds. Per-pupil expenditures for instruction are used in preference to total per-pupil spending because many Texas districts spend lavishly on extracurricular events. Our concern is academic performance, so the spending measure should be based on classroom instruction. Education is personnel intensive, and most spending pays salaries of teachers and other staff. Higher salaries are perceived in economic theory as a way to attract better qualified persons to a profession (Hanushek and Pace 1995). Finally, state aid can be used to compensate for inequities in local tax bases. Although Texas is not a state known for redistributive educational policies, and has a long history in court on this issue (*San Antonio*

---

[5]Median family income in the school district, when included in Table 4.2, is unrelated to educational performance. Our measure of low income is the percentage of students who are eligible for free or reduced-price meals in the school lunch program.

Independent School District v. *Rodriguez*, 1973; *Edgewood Independent School District* v. *Kirby*, 1989; see also Texas Research League 1986; Accountable Cost Advisory Committee 1986; Weiher 1988), greater funds from state governments can compensate for a meager local tax base. All relationships should be positive.

Education policies are adopted with the intent to influence student performance. Three such policies deal with the learning environment. Students cannot learn if they are absent from school; as a result, many districts have adopted policies to encourage and even to compel students to attend classes. The measure we use is the average percentage of students who attend school, although this might also be an environmental variable measuring commitment to education by students or their families. Class size is also perceived as relevant to student performance. Although many studies indicate that only major changes in class size are effective, schools with smaller class sizes should have an advantage at the margin (see Pate-Bain et al. 1992; Nye et al. 1992; Hedges and Greenwald 1996; Hanushek 1996, p. 54). The measure is the number of students per teacher in the district. Finally, gifted classes are generally conceded to be the best education that a school system offers (see DeHaan 1963 for an early exposition of accelerated learning programs for gifted students). The number of students admitted to gifted classes varies greatly across districts (0 to 24 percent in these Texas districts), and greater access should result in better performance. Attendance and gifted classes should be positively related to performance, and class size should be negatively related.

Teacher-based reforms are a key element in many efforts to improve performance. Two teacher measures are included—experience and certification. Experienced teachers should have an advantage in teaching because they have gained the practical experience necessary for effective teaching. Countering this argument is the idea that teacher training has improved in recent years so that less experienced teachers might actually be better able to teach students than has previously been believed.[6] The measure is the average years of teacher experience of the faculty. Regardless of experience, well-trained teachers are a necessity; one indicator of a lack of training is the need to grant temporary specialist certification to teachers. Our measure is the percentage of teachers who have received temporary certification as subject specialists; this variable should be negatively linked to performance.

---

[6] According to the *National Education Goals Report: Building a Nation of Learners*, 1996, the training of teachers is expected to continue to improve to the point that new teachers, and those seeking to become teachers in graduate teaching programs, will have access to a number of programs ". . . for the continued improvement of their professional skills and the opportunity to acquire the knowledge and skills needed to instruct and prepare all American students for the next century" (xv). Although these opportunities will not be restricted to new and relatively inexperienced teachers, such improvements in training and professional development might very well close or even eliminate any "experience gap" in teacher quality between those with many years of experience and those with less.

64   *Jeff Gill, Kenneth J. Meier*

4.3 SWLS Findings

The standard linear model results for all districts (no weights) are shown in Table 4.1, which will be considered our base of comparison and all other results will be viewed relative to it. These ordinary least squares (OLS) results are fairly predictable. In terms of environment, average student performance drops as the student body has relatively more low-income students, black students, and Latino students. Money seems to matter only marginally. Teacher salaries are positively associated with student pass rates, but money spent on instruction or state aid is not shown to be related to performance given these data and this model. The non-teacher policies are all in the predicted direction, with positive relationships between performance and both attendance and gifted classes and a negative relationship for class size. There is no evidence to support teacher noncertification or experience as affecting student performance.

Before conducting any SWAT analysis, the analyst should always look at a graph that compares fitted values from the model to actual observed outcome variable values to see whether the data show any problematic patterns as illustrated in Chapter 1. Figure 4.1 shows a plot with panels displaying the linear fit versus observed outcome variable, a residual dependence plot (the fitted values versus the residuals), and a plot of the residuals against the quantiles of a

Table 4.1   Ordinary Least Squares Model

	Outcome Variable = Exam Pass Rates			
	Explanatory Variable	Coefficient	Std. Error	95% CI
	Intercept	−35.7455	29.2202	[−93.0167: 21.5257]
Environment	Percent Low Income	−0.2931	0.0374	[−0.3664:−0.2198]
	Percent Black	−0.2307	0.0346	[−0.2985:−0.1629]
	Percent Latino	−0.1146	0.0262	[−0.1660:−0.0633]
Financial	Instruction Funds	0.0004	0.0018	[−0.0032: 0.0039]
	Teacher Salaries	0.0012	0.0004	[0.0005: 0.0020]
	Percent State Aid	0.0303	0.0246	[−0.0179: 0.0786]
Policy	Attendance	0.9187	0.2934	[0.3437: 1.4938]
	Gifted Classes	0.1985	0.0996	[0.0032: 0.3937]
	Class Size	−0.9083	0.3370	[−1.5689:−0.2478]
Teachers	Noncertified	−0.1256	0.0699	[−0.2626: 0.0114]
	Experience	−0.0006	0.2267	[−0.4450: 0.4437]

Adjusted $R^2 = 0.57$
$F = 69.33$ on 11 and 522 degrees of freedom
Residual Standard Error = 7.153 on 522 degrees of freedom

4 Substantively Weighted Analytical Techniques for Successes and Failures: SWLS & GSRLS   65

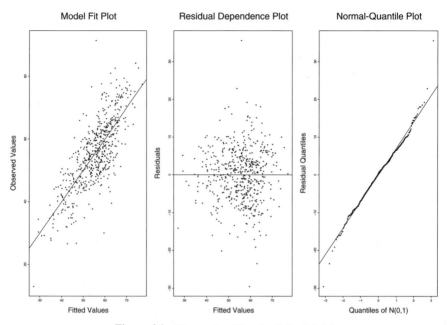

Figure 4.1 Diagnostics: Education Policy Model

normal distribution. In a plot of fitted versus observed values (left panel), indications of problems are nonlinear trends, heteroscedastic patterns such as increasing spread with level, and "gaps" in data. The residual dependence plot (center plot) is useful for detecting heteroscedasticity. Although this plot is nearly the same as the plot of fitted versus observed values, the different scale and horizontal orientation sometimes make it easier to visually detect potential problems. The right panel shows a plot of (ordered) residuals against the (ordered) quantiles of a normal distribution with mean zero and variance one. If the residuals are nearly on the line, then they are approximately normally distributed. A pronounced inverted "S" shape would imply excessively heavy tails and thus some cause for concern. In the case of these data, none of these problems is apparent.

The first type of district we look at is the performance optimizer; this type includes all districts that score better than average when the outcome variables are considered. The selection criterion is all districts with Studentized residuals greater than 0.7 in the standard linear regression. To indicate how these high performers differ from the other districts, we run 20 regressions (the first one is just an unweighted starting point) setting the weight equal to 1 for high performers and decreasing the weight for other districts in increments of 0.05 until the final weight is 0.05.[7] Thus in the terminology of Chapter 3, $\alpha = 0.484$, $\beta = 0.05$.

Table 4.2 shows the final weighted results for these organizations that perform better than expected. The first apparent difference is that money seems to matter for these districts, not just teachers' salaries but per-capita instructional money and state aid as well. Unlike the average districts, high-performing districts appear to get more out of their instructional money and more out of the discretionary money that comes from state government. Only two other differences exist; gifted classes are not related to student performance in these districts, and noncertified teachers are negatively related to performance. A simple comparison of "significance" often is misleading because the individual slopes can change dramatically. For example, the coefficient for Latino students is only half the size of that for the average districts, suggesting that Latino students in high-performing districts do not have as negative an impact on student scores. The logical inference is that these districts might well be using more effective instructional methods for Latino students (more on this relationship below). Another possibility is that these Latino students are somehow more advantaged than Latino students in other districts.

Table 4.2   SWLS, Performance Optimizers

| | Outcome Variable = Exam Pass Rates | | | |
Explanatory Variable		Coefficient	Std. Error	95% CI
	Intercept	−17.3815	18.8670	[−54.3609: 19.5978]
Environment	Percent Low Income	−0.3793	0.0324	[−0.4428:−0.3159]
	Percent Black	−0.2232	0.0287	[−0.2795:−0.1670]
	Percent Latino	−0.0661	0.0235	[−0.1123:−0.0200]
Financial	Instruction Funds	0.0042	0.0016	[0.0011: 0.0073]
	Teacher Salaries	0.0009	0.0003	[0.0003: 0.0015]
	Percent State Aid	0.0611	0.0205	[0.0209: 0.1013]
Policy	Attendance	0.8377	0.1807	[0.4836: 1.1918]
	Gifted Classes	0.1624	0.0932	[−0.0202: 0.3450]
	Class Size	−1.1259	0.2843	[−1.6832:−0.5686]
Teachers	Noncertified	−0.1686	0.0544	[−0.2751:−0.0620]
	Experience	0.1270	0.1781	[−0.222: 0.4760]

Adjusted $R^2 = 0.72$
$F = 123.7847$ qn 11 and 522 degrees of freedom
Residual Standard Error $= 3.040519$

---

[7]The size of the increment is a matter of choice; with many cases, one can run the process to end up with a smaller final weight.

4 Substantively Weighted Analytical Techniques for Successes and Failures: SWLS & GSRLS

One learns about administrative systems not just from studying how they succeed but also from studying how they fail. In fact, failures might be more informative than successes about how a system works (Simon 1957). The failure districts are defined as those with a jackknifed residual of less than -0.7 from the OLS regression—that is, districts that perform less well than expected given constraints and inputs. The final weighted regression for the failure districts is shown in Table 4.3. The coefficients differ from those of both the average districts and the performance-optimizing districts. In terms of financial variables, there is evidence that only teacher salaries appear related to student performance. The policy implication is that these districts might not be helped simply by a greater influx of money for instruction or money from the state. Some districts might be helped, but in general these failure districts probably will not. Attendance and gifted classes remain important, but class size drops from the list. Again, this result suggests that these districts might be unable to take advantage of reductions in class size.

A risk-averse bureaucracy seeks to avoid failures; it seeks to satisfice (Simon 1947) rather than to take large risks that might generate serious problems for the organization. The notion of a risk-averse bureaucracy is one that treats failing (bad performance relative to inputs) as the most serious problem. Within SWLS, this idea can be operationalized as the reverse of the failures' regression. That is, one should gradually downweight the failures and leave the average-performing

Table 4.3   SWLS, Failures Model

		Outcome Variable = Exam Pass Rates		
	Explanatory Variable	Coefficient	Std. Error	95% CI
	Intercept	-89.4018	29.9271	$[-148.0589{:}-30.7447]$
Environment	Percent Low Income	-0.1942	0.0256	$[-0.2444{:}\ -0.1441]$
	Percent Black	-0.2464	0.0273	$[-0.2999{:}\ -0.1930]$
	Percent Latino	-0.1771	0.0175	$[-0.2113{:}\ -0.1429]$
Financial	Instruction Funds	0.0017	0.0015	$[-0.0013{:}\ \ \ 0.0047]$
	Teacher Salaries	0.0012	0.0003	$[\ 0.0007{:}\ \ \ 0.0018]$
	Percent State Aid	0.0309	0.0190	$[-0.0063{:}\ \ \ 0.0681]$
Policy	Attendance	1.2404	0.2971	$[\ 0.6582{:}\ \ \ 1.8226]$
	Gifted Classes	0.2341	0.0862	$[\ 0.0651{:}\ \ \ 0.4032]$
	Class Size	-0.2893	0.2895	$[-0.8566{:}\ \ \ 0.2781]$
Teachers	Noncertified	-0.1412	0.0616	$[-0.2619{:}\ -0.0205]$
	Experience	0.0885	0.1840	$[-0.2722{:}\ \ \ 0.4492]$

Adjusted $R^2 = 0.65$
$F = 90.48882$ on 11 and 522 degrees of freedom
Residual Standard Error $= 3.008265$

bureaucracies at the starting weight of 1.0. Quite clearly, being risk averse is not a bad situation since the risk-averse districts are not all that different from the performance optimizers (compare Table 4.4 to Table 4.2). There is no evidence that they get any positive benefits from more instructional money, but other than that the same relationships are 95% CI bounded away from zero for risk averse and performance-optimizing bureaucracies. The slopes are at times different across the models in Tables 4.2, 4.3, and 4.4 which provides additional information valuable to the organization.

Perhaps the best way to examine four separate regressions at the same time is with a multiregression barplot. The individual bars of the barplot are drawn to reflect the size of the coefficients with the shading of the bars indicating statistical significance (again, p-values are used purely for visual convenience). Figure 4.2 shows at a quick glance the major differences between performance-optimizing agencies, failures, and risk-averse agencies. Note that since each explanatory variable is measured in its own distinct units, within-barplot (rows) comparisons are not meaningful. In addition, one should pay close attention to the scale of the Y-axis. Next to each barplot is a quantile plot of the residuals of the corresponding weighted regression model against quantiles of the standard normal distribution. This plot provides immediate visual detection of a departure from an important assumption of the linear model. The relatively tight fit and shape of the residuals suggest no heteroscedasticity problems.

Table 4.4   SWLS, Risk-Averse Model

	Outcome Variable = Exam Pass Rates			
Explanatory Variable		Coefficient	Std. Error	95% CI
	Intercept	−4.2609	20.6067	[−44.6501: 36.1282]
Environment	Percent Low Income	−0.3724	0.0306	[−0.4323:−0.3124]
	Percent Black	−0.2109	0.0267	[−0.2632:−0.1587]
	Percent Latino	−0.0687	0.0218	[−0.1115:−0.0259]
Financial	Instruction Funds	0.0003	0.0013	[−0.0023: 0.0028]
	Teacher Salaries	0.0013	0.0003	[0.0007: 0.0018]
	Percent State Aid	0.0433	0.0190	[0.0062: 0.0805]
Policy	Attendance	0.7269	0.2078	[0.3197: 1.1341]
	Gifted Classes	0.1155	0.0732	[−0.028: 0.2589]
	Class Size	−1.4706	0.2489	[−1.9585:−0.9828]
Teachers	Noncertified	−0.1234	0.0510	[−0.2234:−0.0234]
	Experience	−0.0260	0.1711	[−0.3615: 0.3094]

Adjusted $R^2 = 0.75$
$F = 141.4527$ on 11 and 522 degrees of freedom
Residual Standard Error = 4.697196

4 Substantively Weighted Analytical Techniques for Successes and Failures: SWLS & GSRLS

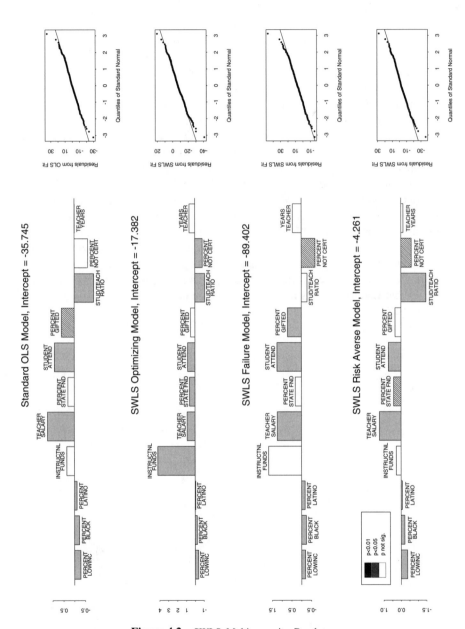

Figure 4.2 SWLS, Multiregression Barplot

Tables 4.2, 4.3, and 4.4 are only the final weighted regressions. Those results are the most useful in SWLS, but the intermediate regressions also can reveal interesting patterns. One major difference between the performance optimizers and the failures is the relationship between percentage of Latino students and test scores. If we treat the OLS regression coefficients as equal to one and then plot the optimizing and the failure coefficients from each regression on a graph, as in Figure 4.3, the pattern of relationships becomes quickly obvious. For the failures, the size of the Latino student coefficient gradually increases in magnitude until it is 54% larger than the OLS coefficient. In contrast, the optimizers' coefficient shrinks in magnitude until it is only 60% of the OLS coefficient. These results indicate substantively that a one percent increase in Latino students has less than one-third the negative impact in the optimizing districts as in the failure districts. This situation does not result because the optimizing districts have fewer Latino students; in fact, they have slightly more (32.2% compared to 30.0%; the average districts have 31.3%). Thus, an examination of the programs targeted at Latino students in the optimizing districts could well provide important technical knowledge toward improving the performance of Latino students. In investigating this relationship, the analyst should verify that Latino students in these districts are not different from those in other districts.

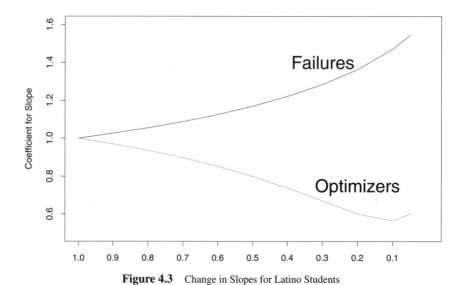

Figure 4.3 Change in Slopes for Latino Students

4.4 GSRLS Results

SWLS was developed with the limitations of the technical base of public administration in mind. It can generally be performed with any statistical package that can do weighted least squares (that is, virtually all of them). The intuitive appeal of the technique, however, should not blind one to the fact that several criteria in the process are essentially arbitrary. Using a Studentized residual of 0.7 was proposed by Meier and Keiser (1996) so that enough cases would be designated high performing that the results would not reflect the idiosyncrasies of a single agency or two (their dataset had only 50 cases). With larger datasets, a Studentized residual of 0.7 is not especially exclusive. In our current example, the criterion selects more than 120 districts. Some analysts might well want to be more selective (see Chapter 5).

The weighting criterion, gradually decreasing by 0.1, was proposed simply because it was tractable. This chapter goes a step further to downweight in increments of 0.05. Different weighting concerns could be used in appropriate situations. Also, SWLS does not reexamine the jackknifed residuals after the first regression; that is, it does not reweight subsequent regressions based on the results of the previous regression. Although this method has the advantage of reducing the number of steps, it has the disadvantage that one case will remain weighted highly when it may be only marginally better than the average case. A general approach (Gill 1997; and Chapter 3) to substantively weighted least squares can address some of these limitations by allowing any threshold level for determination of which externally Studentized residuals constitute outliers, and any desired number of iterations before producing the final reweighted analysis. To keep the process as identical as possible, we replicate our analyses with generalized substantively reweighted least squares (GSRLS) using the same number of iterations and the same size increments. The results are presented in Tables 4.5, 4.6, and 4.7.

4.5 Differences Between SWLS and GSRLS

In general, the reweighting algorithm (GSRLS) did not give radically different results than the constant-weight algorithm (SWLS) for these data. This generalization applies to the applications where unsuccessful and typical cases were downweighted (optimizing model), where successful and typical cases were downweighted (failure model), and where only failure cases were downweighted (risk-averse model). The comparison yields no dramatic cases such as the switching of signs on variable coefficients where the coefficients have 95% confidence intervals bounded away from zero.

Table 4.5 GSRLS, Performance Optimizers Model

| | Outcome Variable = Exam Pass Rates | | | |
Explanatory Variable		Coefficient	Std. Error	95% CI
	Intercept	3.2174	24.7320	[−45.2574: 51.6921]
Environment	Percent Low Income	−0.3943	0.0460	[−0.4844:−0.3041]
	Percent Black	−0.2409	0.0399	[−0.3191:−0.1627]
	Percent Latino	−0.0610	0.0320	[−0.1237: 0.0016]
Financial	Instruction Funds	0.0053	0.0020	[0.0013: 0.0093]
	Teacher Salaries	0.0007	0.0004	[−0.0001: 0.0015]
	Percent State Aid	0.0700	0.0257	[0.0196: 0.1204]
Policy	Attendance	0.6698	0.2315	[0.2160: 1.1237]
	Gifted Classes	0.1909	0.1264	[−0.0569: 0.4387]
	Class Size	−1.3100	0.3688	[−2.0328:−0.5871]
Teachers	Noncertified	−0.1585	0.0701	[−0.2959:−0.0211]
	Experience	0.1964	0.2480	[−0.2897: 0.6825]

Adjusted $R^2 = 0.57$
$F = 62.51117$ on 11 and 522 degrees of freedom
Residual Standard Error = 2.954563
Unweighted Cases: First Iteration = 125, Last Iteration = 58

Table 4.6 GSRLS, Failure Model

| | Outcome Variable = Exam Pass Rates | | | |
Explanatory Variable		Coefficient	Std. Error	95% CI
	Intercept	−81.8246	38.8950	[−158.0588:−5.5904]
Environment	Percent Low Income	−0.1627	0.0307	[−0.2228:−0.1027]
	Percent Black	−0.2478	0.0326	[−0.3117:−0.1839]
	Percent Latino	−0.1999	0.0213	[−0.2416:−0.1582]
Financial	Instruction Funds	0.0027	0.0022	[−0.0017: 0.0070]
	Teacher Salaries	0.0013	0.0004	[0.0005: 0.0021]
	Percent State Aid	0.0428	0.0241	[−0.0043: 0.0900]
Policy	Attendance	1.0576	0.3954	[0.2826: 1.8326]
	Gifted Classes	0.2678	0.1147	[0.0430: 0.4925]
	Class Size	−0.0463	0.3959	[−0.8222: 0.7297]
Teachers	Noncertified	−0.1462	0.0917	[−0.3259: 0.0335]
	Experience	0.0758	0.2592	[−0.4322: 0.5838]

Adjusted $R^2 = 0.55$
$F = 57.53106$ on 11 and 522 degrees of freedom
Residual Standard Error = 2.943185
Unweighted Cases: First Iteration = 126, Last Iteration = 58

4 *Substantively Weighted Analytical Techniques for Successes and Failures: SWLS & GSRLS* 73

Table 4.7 GSRLS, Risk-Averse Model

Explanatory Variable		Coefficient	Std. Error	95% CI
	Outcome Variable = Exam Pass Rates			
	Intercept	3.8388	21.4250	[−38.1541: 45.8318]
Environment	Percent Low Income	−0.4276	0.0325	[−0.4913:−0.3640]
	Percent Black	−0.1917	0.0280	[−0.2465:−0.1369]
	Percent Latino	−0.0250	0.0231	[−0.0704: 0.0203]
Financial	Instruction Funds	−0.0001	0.0013	[−0.0027: 0.0025]
	Teacher Salaries	0.0012	0.0003	[0.0006: 0.0017]
	Percent State Aid	0.0481	0.0196	[0.0098: 0.0865]
Policy	Attendance	0.6985	0.2142	[0.2786: 1.1184]
	Gifted Classes	0.0814	0.0808	[−0.0769: 0.2398]
	Class Size	−1.6884	0.2535	[−2.1852:−1.1915]
Teachers	Noncertified	−0.0860	0.0540	[−0.1918: 0.0198]
	Experience	0.0738	0.1813	[−0.2816: 0.4292]

Adjusted $R^2 = 0.73$
$F = 126.7176$ on 11 and 522 degrees of freedom
Residual Standard Error $= 4.771231$
Unweighted Cases: First Iteration $= 408$, Last Iteration $= 379$

There are some important differences, however, between the SWLS and GSRLS approaches. The primary difference is that there is an overall reduction in statistical significance for the GSRLS models: fewer of the 95% confidence intervals for the coefficients are bounded away from zero. In a sense, it is harder to be "significant" with the reweighting procedure. For example, the coefficient for the percent Latino variable has 95% confidence interval bounded away from zero in the SWLS optimizing model, [−0.1123:−0.0200], but not in the GSRLS optimizing model, [−0.1237:0.0016].[8] The variable for average teacher's salary shows this same effect. We add the caution, however, that confidence interval thresholds (99%, 95%, 90%,...) are as arbitrary as p-value thresholds or "stars." However, confidence intervals are vastly superior in that the expression of uncertainty at any of these given levels is the provided interval width. Furthermore, arbitrary significance levels are also associated with parameter estimates rather than the more qualitative indicators that SWAT analysis generates.

In the risk-averse models (Tables 4.4 and 4.7), percent of noncertified teachers changes from bounded away from zero (SWLS) to bounding zero (GSRLS). There are no cases where the significance is improved by the GSRLS model over the

---

[8]Substantively, this finding could be important since it underscores our discussion of how high-performing districts teach Latino students.

74   *Jeff Gill, Kenneth J. Meier*

SWLS model. Having said this, we note that the majority of results are reasonably similar with these data whether reweighting or not.

Figures 4.2 and 4.4 highlight the model differences by graphically comparing the model coefficients while simultaneously indicating statistical significance (here we resort to ranges of p-values, indicated by the shading of the bars, purely for graphical convenience). These multiregression barplots allow (vertical) comparison of coefficients under different modeling procedures. Note again, however, *that horizontally comparing effect magnitudes within models is inappropriate, as the magnitude of each coefficient is expressed in its own units of measurement.*

The variable for percent of state aid shows some interesting behavior in both the SWLS and GSRLS models. It has a 95% confidence interval bounding zero in the OLS model and the failure models, but has a 95% confidence interval bounded away from zero in the optimizing models and risk-averse models. This distinction points out the danger in applying OLS results to all prescriptive scenarios: there is no evidence here that increasing the percentage of state aid helps poorly performing schools. Perhaps the problems that affect test scores in these schools are more fundamental than funding and allocation issues. Alternatively, these districts might perform poorly because they do not use state aid effectively.

In the SWLS approach, the failure model is the only one in which the class size coefficient is not 95% CI bounded away from zero, which suggests that effective management of this ratio (number of students per teacher) is not a promising strategy for this type of district. Although this finding is counterintuitive, it suggests that the quality of teaching at the poorly performing schools could be a key causal latent variable or that class size is simply swamped by the other factors. Note that relying on the traditional linear model would not have highlighted this important subtlety in the data. Looked at from the opposite perspective, the instructional funds coefficient is 95% CI bounded away from zero only in the optimizing model (both SWLS and GSRLS), and therefore likely to be important only for administrators of districts that are already high performers.

A central question of this part of the analysis is: what does it mean when there are changing levels of "significance" and concurrently changing coefficient values between two comparison models (i.e., optimizing versus risk averse or failure)? For instance, percent noncertified teachers is not 95% CI bounded away from zero in the OLS model but is 95% CI bounded away from zero for every other model (SWLS and GSRLS except GSRLS failure and risk-averse).[9] This is because the effects are masked when all types of cases are considered with equal weights. This is evidence that the SWAT approach enables researchers to understand the prescriptive impact of explanatory variable levels in a more *substantive* way. The OLS model would have provided administrators at poorly performing schools the wrong advice as to how to improve their future results. Note that the definition

---

[9]Note that this finding is somewhat reminiscent of Simpson's paradox.

4 Substantively Weighted Analytical Techniques for Successes and Failures: SWLS & GSRLS   75

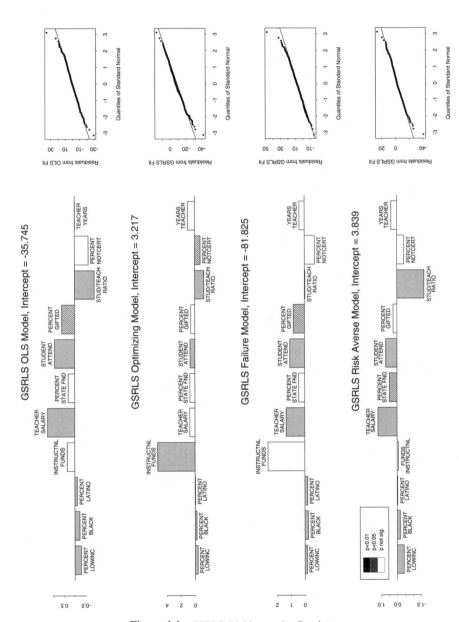

Figure 4.4 GSRLS, Multiregression Barplot

of "significant" here corresponds more accurately to "further distinct from zero in confidence interval measure" in the final SWAT analysis with regard to the selected subset of unweighted cases. The word does *not* imply that the population parameters are estimated to be distinct from zero. This distinction is the essence of SWAT's concentration on cases of interest and their prescriptive information rather than on the typical case indicated by the mean.

In all models, there are highly reliable variables that policy makers have little control over: percent low income, percent black students, and percent Latino students. Their coefficients in the model have 95% confidence intervals bounded away from zero except GSRLS optimizers and risk-averse. Since administrators cannot manipulate these levels, prescriptive guidance should generally be focused elsewhere. At the same time, the impact of these variables does vary across the different types of districts. This variance could well result from specific educational processes that are not in our model. For example, a district with an excellent bilingual education program could generate a smaller regression coefficient for percent Latino students.

The variable percent enrolled in gifted classes is 95% CI bounded away from zero for the OLS model, but not for the optimizing or risk-averse model (SWLS and GSRLS). This effect is analogous to spurious controlled variables in that the effect disappears when the control is implemented. Since the GSRLS models are in effect controlling for a specified phenomenon, residual behavior, the analogy is appropriate. The central question about the percent enrolled in gifted classes variable may be one of causality. If a school is low performing, then the effect of increasing availability of gifted classes is more dramatic. This chain of causality can be considered a partial explanation for the spurious effect: low-performing schools can improve the percent passing through increased emphasis on gifted classes if they have potentially gifted students to fill them. Conversely, high-performing schools may have already determined the correct proportion of gifted classes to offer.[10]

Finally, it is crucial to evaluate the variance of the residuals to ensure that unwelcome heteroscedasticity has not been introduced by the GSRLS process. As mentioned before, a residual dependence plot provides an intuitive way to visually assess such effects. Figure 4.5 shows the residual dependence plots for each of the GSRLS models developed in this section. There is evidence of a very small number of outliers in the tails of the normal-quantile plot, but no visual indication of serious heteroscedasticity in the three models.

---

[10]This explanation assumes the size of gifted programs is equal to the district's supply of students capable of performing at that level. An average district with fewer classes than needed could be detrimentally affected. Some literature assumes most students would benefit from gifted classes (see Meier and Stewart 1991). That assumption currently lacks empirical support.

4 Substantively Weighted Analytical Techniques for Successes and Failures: SWLS & GSRLS 77

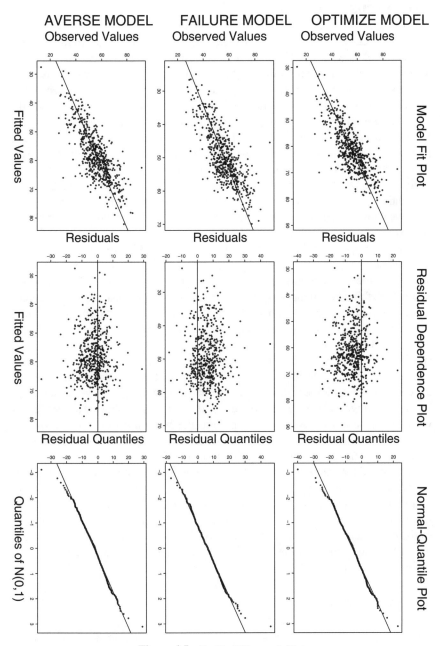

Figure 4.5 Residual Diagnostic Plots

4.6 Discussion

The core focus of this chapter is to show that more than one group of interest can be isolated with SWAT analysis. We also show that such analysis may reveal interesting differences in how these groups use the resources at their disposal. It is irrational to think that superior bureaucracies manipulate factors in the same way as typical or inferior ones. SWAT addresses the question of exactly what differences in input factors are important in distinguishing performance. We looked at four general classes of educational bureaucracies: typical (OLS model), superior (optimizing model), poor (failure model), and trepidant (risk-averse model), but the real point behind this chapter is that the SWAT-enabled analyst is free to define his or her own definition of a group of interest. In this way, those studying the effect of varying factor use in public management settings can reveal interesting nuances in the data that are hidden by standard linear model analysis.

SWAT is a set of flexible tools that should be included in every public management scholar's repertoire of skills. It is a general way to add values into statistical analysis by focusing attention on key cases designated by the analyst: performance optimizers, failures, equitable agencies, or any other value that can be measured. By its emphasis on key cases, it can bridge the academic–practitioner gap. When coupled with in-depth case studies of selected key programs or agencies, it offers the potential for significant gains in the efficiency of process analyses by specifying which cases and which variables to examine.

An important benefit of using SWAT tools is that effects that are masked or distorted in standard linear models for specific case typologies (high-performing, low-performing, risk-averse) can be revealed. This chapter showed several cases where the prescriptive recommendation from OLS regression would have provided *exactly the wrong recipe* for improvement for some type of school system. Thus SWAT techniques are a powerful addition to any public manager's toolkit.

A substantial portion of this chapter compared SWLS with GSRLS. In general, the results were similar, suggesting that the use of SWLS, the less demanding option in terms of technique, will serve public management adequately. At the same time, we need to stress that GSRLS is the more conservative technique statistically and, therefore, is to be preferred. The solution quite clearly is to get the GSRLS algorithm included in the widely available software packages.

4.7 References

Accountable Cost Advisory Committee. 1986. *Accountable Cost Study and Recommendations of the Accountable Cost Advisory Committee to the State Board of Education.* Austin, TX: Texas Education Agency.

Barzelay, Michael. 1992. *Breaking Through Bureaucracy*. Berkeley: University of California Press.

Boyer, Brian D. 1973. *Cities Destroyed for Cash*. Chicago: Follett Publishing.

Burtless, Gary. 1996. *Does Money Matter? The Effect of School Resources on Student Achievement and Adult Success*. Washington: Brookings Institution.

Coleman, James S. 1986. "School Districts and Student Achievement in British Columbia: A Preliminary Analysis." *Canadian Journal of Education* 11: 509–21.

DeHaan, Robert F. 1963. *Accelerated Learning Programs*. Washington, D.C.: Center for Applied Research in Education, Inc.

Edgewood Independent School District v. *Kirby*. Texas SupCt, No. C-8353 (1989).

Fernandez, Ricardo R., and William Velez. 1985. "Race, Color, and Language in the Changing Public Schools." In *Urban Ethnicity in the United States*, edited by Lionel Maldonado and Joan Moore. Beverly Hills, CA: Sage, 107–40.

Fuller, Bruce, Costanza Eggers-Pierola, Susan D. Holloway, Xiaoyam Liang, and Marylee F. Rambaud. 1996. "Rich Culture, Poor Markets: Why Do Latino Parents Forego Preschooling?" *Teachers College Record* 97: 400–18.

Gill, Jeff. 1997. "Generalized Substantively Reweighted Least Squares Regression." *Political Methodology WWW Site*. http://polmeth.calpoly.edu.

Hanushek, Eric A. 1996. "School Resources and Student Performance." In *Does Money Matter? The Effect of School Resources on Student Achievement and Adult Success*, edited by Gary Burtless. Washington, D.C.: Brookings Institution.

Hanushek, Eric A. 1994. "Money Might Matter Somewhere: A Response to Hedges, Laine, and Greenwald." *Educational Researcher* 23, 5–8.

Hanushek, Eric A. 1989. "The Impact of Differential Expenditures on School Performance." *Educational Researcher* 23: 45–65.

Hanushek, Eric A. 1986. "The Economics of Schooling: Production and Efficiency in Public Schools." *Journal of Economic Literature* 24: 1141–77.

Hanushek, Eric A. 1981. "Throwing Money at Schools." *Journal of Policy Analysis and Management* 1: 19–41.

Hanushek, Eric A., and Richard R. Pace. 1995. "Who Chooses to Teach (and Why?)" *Economics of Education Review* 14: 107–17.

Hedges, Larry V., and Rob Greenwald. 1996. "Have Times Changed? The Relation Between School Resources and Student Performance." In *Does Money Matter? The Effect of School Resources on Student Achievement and Adult Success*, edited by Gary Burtless. Washington, D.C.: Brookings Institution.

Hedges, Larry V., R. D. Laine, and Rob Greenwald. 1994. "Does Money Matter? A Meta-Analysis of Studies of the Effects of Differential School Inputs on Student Outcomes." *Educational Researcher* 23: 383–93.

Heimann, C. F. Larry. 1993. "Understanding the *Challenger* Disaster: Organizational Structure and the Design of Reliable Systems." *American Political Science Review* 87: 421–35.

Johnston, Kenneth B. 1993. *Beyond Bureaucracy: A Blueprint and Vision for Government That Works*. Homewood, IL: Business One Irwin.

80 *Jeff Gill, Kenneth J. Meier*

Kaufman, Herbert. 1981. *The Administrative Behavior of Federal Bureau Chiefs.* Washington, D.C.: Brookings Institution.

Kickbusch, Karla. 1985. "Minority Students in Mathematics: The Reading Skill Connection." *Sociological Inquiry* 55: 402.

LaPiere, Richard T. 1965. *Social Change.* New York: McGraw-Hill.

Mann, Dale, and Deborah Inman. 1984. "Improving Education Within Existing Resources: The Instructionally Effective Schools' Approach." *Journal of Education Finance* 10: 256–69.

Meier, Kenneth J., and Lael R. Keiser. 1996. "Public Administration as a Science of the Artificial: A Methodology for Prescription." *Public Administration Review* 56: 459–66.

Meier, Kenneth J., and Joseph Stewart, Jr. 1991. *The Politics of Hispanic Education.* Albany, NY: State University of New York Press.

Meier, Kenneth J., Robert D. Wrinkle, and J. L. Polinard. 1999. "Equity and Excellence in Education: A Substantively Reweighted Least Squares Analysis." *American Review of Public Administration* 29: 5–18.

Moore, Elsie G. J., and A. Wade Smith. 1986. "Sex and Race Differences in Mathematics Aptitude: Effects of Schooling." *Sociological Perspectives* 29: 77.

Murray, Sheila E. 1995. *Two Essays on the Distribution of Education Resources and Outcomes.* Unpublished Ph.D. dissertation, Department of Economics, University of Maryland.

Murray, Sheila E., William N. Evans, and Robert M. Schwab. 1995. "Money Matters After All: Evidence from Panel Data on the Effects of School Resources." University of Kentucky and University of Maryland working paper: The Martin School.

National Education Goals Panel. 1996. *The National Education Goals Report: Building a Nation of Learners.* Washington, D.C.: U.S. Government Printing Office.

Necochea, Juan, and Zullmara Cune. 1996. "A Case Study of Within District School Funding Inequities." *Equity and Excellence in Education* 29: 69–77.

Nye, B. A.; J. Boyd-Zacharias, B. D. Fulton, and M. P. Wallenhorst. 1992. "Smaller Classes Really Are Better." *American School Board Journal* May: 31–33.

Osborne, David, and Ted Gaebler. 1992. *Re-Inventing Government: How the Entrepreneurial Spirit Is Transforming the Public Sector.* Reading, MA: Addison-Wesley.

Pate-Bain, H.; C. M. Achilles, J. Boyd-Zacharias, and B. McKenna. 1992. "Class Size Does Make a Difference." *Phi Delta Kappan* November: 253–56.

Report of the National Performance Review. 1993. Washington, D.C.: U.S. Government Printing Office.

Romzek, Barbara, and Melvin J. Dubnick. 1987. "Accountability in the Public Sector: Lessons for the *Challenger* Tragedy." *Public Administration Review* 47: 227-38.

Rong, Xue Lan, and Linda Grant. 1992. "Ethnicity, Generation, and School Attainment of Asians, Hispanics, and Non-Hispanic Whites." *Sociological Quarterly* 33: 625.

Rossmiller, Richard A. 1987. "Achieving Equity and Effectiveness in Schooling." *Journal of Education Finance* 12: 561–77.

San Antonio Independent School District v. *Rodriguez.* 411 U.S. 1 (1973).

Simon, Herbert. 1947. *Administrative Behavior.* New York: Free Press.

Simon, Herbert. 1981 (1957). *The Sciences of the Artificial*. Cambridge, MA: MIT Press.

Sjoberg, Gideon, Richard A. Brymer, and Buford Farris. 1966. "Bureaucracy and the Lower Class." *Sociology and Social Research* (April) 325–27.

Smith, Kevin B., and Kenneth J. Meier. 1994. "Bureaucrats, Markets, and Schools." *Public Administration Review* 54: 511–58.

Texas Research League. 1986. *Bench Marks for 1986–87 School District Budgets in Texas*. Austin, TX: Texas Research League.

Walberg, Herbert J., and William J. Fowler. 1987. "Expenditure and Size Efficiencies of Public School Districts." *Educational Researcher* 16: 5–13.

Weiher, Gregory R. 1988. "Why Redistribution Doesn't Work: State Educational Reform Policy and Governmental Decentralization in Texas." *American Politics Quarterly* 16: 193–210.

Wolman, Harold. 1971. *The Politics of Federal Housing*. New York: Dodd, Mead.

Chapter 5

Separating Excellent Agencies from the Good Ones: Pushing the Extremes of the Data Distribution[1]

Jeff Gill, Kenneth J. Meier

5.1 Introduction

Charles Goodsell (1983) characterizes American bureaucracy as similar to a good used car: it is reliable, relatively inexpensive to operate, and generally gives good service. Bureaucracy, in Goodsell's estimation, is the equivalent of Ralph's Pretty Good Grocery in Lake Woebegone. Goodsell's assessment is meant to be an average for American bureaucracy; he recognized, and others have presented information, that American bureaucracies vary a great deal about that mean (Meier 1993; Wolf 1997). With the current public philosophy of neoconservative economics (Lan and Rosenbloom 1992; Osborne and Gaebler 1992), being "pretty good" is unlikely to be good enough to meet the expectations of policy makers and the public. Public administrators can no longer be content to simply distinguish

---

[1] An earlier version of this chapter was presented at the 1998 Midwest Political Science Association annual meetings, Palmer House Hotel, Chicago, IL.

84   *Jeff Gill, Kenneth J. Meier*

the good from the bad and the ugly. What is needed is a way to look at the pretty good agencies and distinguish among that group those that are exceptional, the stars that other organizations can emulate to provide more effective performance.

Two general theories explain why the performance of bureaucracy varies. A general set of approaches, best characterized as open system theory (Thompson 1967; Rourke 1984), argues that some organizations perform better because they are more highly skilled, possess more useful expertise, or use better quality leadership to exploit their environment to a higher degree. Those that do so are more likely to survive because their performance continues to meet or exceed expectations (Downs 1967). Because organizations make decisions by satisficing (Simon 1947), however, even among organizations performing at the highest levels, there will be considerable variation in what they do and how they do it. Also, even agencies advantaged by considerable resources can under-perform relative to their potential *given* those resources. Conversely, an agency with a paucity of resources can outperform reasonable expectations.

A second, more provocative theory of organizational variance and survival is that of Herbert Kaufman (1991). Kaufman argues that organizations survive and flourish not because they do things better than other organizations, but rather because they are lucky. In the Darwinist natural selection of organizations, the survivors are those blessed with favorable and stable environments.[2]

Within the context of either theory, being able to distinguish good (lucky) agencies from exceptional (really lucky) agencies is well worthwhile. At the same time, if high performance can be attributed primarily to factors in an organization's environment, then Kaufman is likely to be correct about why some organizations outperform others;[3] and our attention should shift to the organization's environment and how to structure this environment. If, on the other hand, high performance results because exceptional agencies use environment inputs in better ways than other agencies, the open system's perspective will gain credence.

This chapter, as a result, has both practical and theoretical ends. It uses substantively weighted analytical techniques (SWAT) to focus on performance optimization by agencies. The units of analysis are again 534 school systems in Texas.

---

[2]The logical extension of Kaufman's argument is Chubb and Moe's (1989) suggestion that one should focus on organizational environments and structure them in such a way that they do not make a large number of contradictory demands on the organization. In their study of school choice, Chubb and Moe argue that suburban schools and private schools perform better because they exist in homogeneous environments.

[3]Kaufman could still be wrong if the key organizational skill that is operating is the ability to placate one's environment. As open systems, bureaucracies both respond to their environment and shape the nature of that environment. What might appear to be a highly favorable environment might actually reflect exceptional political and managerial skills. As one illustration, J. Edgar Hoover was able to define the Federal Bureau of Investigation's role in such a way to be able to deal with cases that were highly visible yet easy to solve (bank robbery, kidnapping) and avoid cases that were difficult to solve or corrupting (prohibition, drug abuse); see Poveda (1990). The result of this strategy was a great deal of organizational autonomy and ample resources.

School systems are not only the most prevalent public bureaucracies in the United States, but they also have some relatively objective measures of outputs so that the question of performance can be addressed. First, the chapter presents an education production function where student performance is a function of the school system's environment and various policies and resource allocations. Second, we modify that approach to distinguish excellent districts from those that are merely good. Third, we examine the agencies with these techniques, both illustrating how they can be used for this purpose and addressing the theoretical dispute about how organizations change and adapt. Finally, we discuss additional elements of organizational performance that can be assessed in a similar manner.

5.2 An Education Production Function

School districts are organizations; they receive inputs (resources and students) from their environment and produce outputs (educated students among others). A vast literature has designated a variety of education production functions whereby the outputs of school systems can be evaluated relative to their inputs (Burtless 1996; Smith 1995; Hanushek 1996, 1989, 1986). Because our objective is to contribute to the literature on public organizations rather than to the literature on education policy, our discussion of the education production function and all its possible nuances is brief (for a more elaborate discussion, see Burtless 1996). We are seeking to set up a criterion for evaluation rather than to resolve substantive issues in education policy.

Our outcome variable—that is, the measure of school system outputs—is based on student scores on standardized tests. Texas requires all school districts to administer exams to students in grades 3, 5, 7, 9, and 11 on an annual basis. Our outcome variable is the percentage of students who passed these exams in 1991. The explanatory variables are the same as those used in Chapter 4. This chapter applies SWAT techniques in a somewhat different manner. Rather than substantively weighting the above average cases (or the below average cases; see Chapter 4), the method will gradually change the definition of an above average agency so that it encompasses fewer and fewer agencies. These smaller and smaller subsets of agencies that perform better and better will be the "supermarkets" of agency performers.

5.3 Linear Model Findings

The basic linear model results from the production function analysis for all 534 school districts were provided in Table 4.1 in Chapter 4 and are repeated in Table 5.1 for convenience. These results should be considered the base regression and serve as a standard for comparison. The general predictions of the production

86   *Jeff Gill, Kenneth J. Meier*

Table 5.1   Ordinary Least Squares Model

	Outcome Variable = Exam Pass Rates			
Explanatory Variable		Coefficient	Std. Error	95% CI
	Intercept	−35.7455	29.2202	[−93.0167: 21.5257]
Environment	Percent Low Income	−0.2931	0.0374	[−0.3664:−0.2198]
	Percent Black	−0.2307	0.0346	[−0.2985: −0.1629]
	Percent Latino	−0.1146	0.0262	[−0.1660: −0.0633]
Financial	Instruction Funds (K)	0.3530	0.0018	[−0.0032: 0.0039]
	Teacher Salaries (K)	1.2444	0.0004	[0.0005: 0.0020]
	Percent State Aid	0.0303	0.0246	[−0.0179: 0.0786]
Policy	Attendance	0.9187	0.2934	[0.3437: 1.4938]
	Gifted Classes	0.1985	0.0996	[0.0032: 0.3937]
	Class Size	−0.9083	0.3370	[−1.5689: −0.2478]
Teachers	Noncertified	−0.1256	0.0699	[−0.2626: 0.0114]
	Experience	−0.0006	0.2267	[−0.4450: 0.4437]

Adjusted $R^2 = 0.57$

$F = 69.33$ on 11 and 522 degrees of freedom

Residual Standard Error = 7.153 on 522 degrees of freedom

function model are borne out rather well. Student pass rates are negatively associated with all three environmental factors—low income, black, and Latino students. Financial resources do not fare as well; only teachers' salaries are noticeably related to student performance, although the other two measures are in the predicted direction. The teacher qualification measures are disappointing; both relationships are negative, but neither has a coefficient estimate that is 95% confidence interval (CI) bounded away from zero. Policy measures hold up rather well, with performance being positively related to attendance and gifted classes and negatively related to class size. In addition, each of the policy measure coefficients has a 95% confidence interval bounded away from zero.

5.4 The Pretty Good Agencies

The most basic version of SWAT, substantively weighted least squares (SWLS), takes the jackknifed residuals from the ordinary least squares equation. It then runs a series of regressions, downweighting those cases that do not exceed 0.7. In the first analysis, a series of 19 additional regressions were run and each iteration downweighted the "average cases" by 0.05. In other words, the first weighted regression weighted average cases 0.95 and above average cases 1.0. This iterative

5   *Separating Excellent Agencies from the Good Ones: Extremes of the Data Distribution*   87

process continued until the final regression had respective weights[4] of 0.05 and 1.0. Thus observed differences between Table 5.2 and Table 4.2 are attributable to the difference of $\beta = 20$ used here and $\beta = 10$ used throughout Chapter 4.

Table 5.2 presents the final weighted regression from the SWLS analysis where the jackknifed residual threshold is set at 0.7. Because our selection criterion for above average was 0.7, this regression essentially shows how the "pretty good" differ from the average agencies. One good way to compare the results of these two regressions is with a multiregression barplot (see Figure 5.1, first two rows). First, student performance is now positively and significantly related to instructional monies and percent of state aid (a 95% CI bounded away from zero on the positive side). Second, student performance in the above average agencies is also negatively related to noncertified teachers. Third, the positive relationship between gifted classes and student performance disappears with this model. Quite clearly, the relationships for the above average agencies are different from those for the average agency.

A more precise view of the difference between average agencies and the pretty good ones is shown in Table 5.3, which compares the slopes for the two sets of

Table 5.2   SWLS, The Pretty Good Agencies

	Outcome Variable = Exam Pass Rates			
	Explanatory Variable	Slope	Std. Error	95% CI
	Intercept	−8.4915	20.3821	[−48.4404: 31.4574]
Environment	Percent Low Income	−0.3778	0.0323	[−0.4411:−0.3145]
	Percent Black	−0.2198	0.0287	[−0.2761:−0.1635]
	Percent Latino	−0.0683	0.0235	[−0.1144:−0.0222]
Financial	Instruction Funds	4.3350	1.6056	[1.1880: 7.4820]
	Teacher Salaries	0.8696	0.3011	[0.2794: 1.4598]
	Percent State Aid	0.0601	0.0207	[0.0195: 0.1007]
Policy	Attendance	0.7616	0.1913	[0.3867: 1.1365]
	Gifted Classes	0.1297	0.0943	[−0.0551: 0.3145]
	Class Size	−1.1558	0.2839	[−1.7122:−0.5994]
Teachers	Noncertified	−0.1643	0.0545	[−0.2711:−0.0575]
	Experience	0.0598	0.1808	[−0.2946: 0.4142]

Adjusted $R^2 = 0.72$
$F = 123.78$ on 11 and 522 degrees of freedom
Residual Standard Error = 3.041 on 522 degrees of freedom

---

[4]The analyst can vary these weights either by increasing the size of the increment change and decreasing the number of iterations or by decreasing the size of the incremental change and increasing the number of iterations.

88 Jeff Gill, Kenneth J. Meier

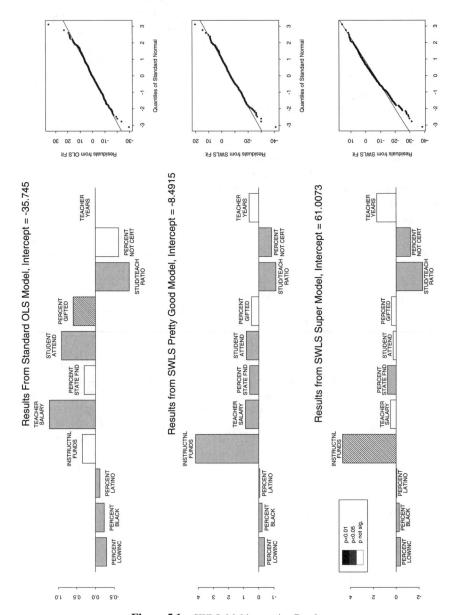

Figure 5.1 SWLS, Multiregression Barplot

5 Separating Excellent Agencies from the Good Ones: Extremes of the Data Distribution

Table 5.3 Average Agencies versus the Pretty Good Ones: Slope Comparison

	Explanatory Variable	All Agencies (OLS)	Pretty Good (SWLS)	Ratio
Environment	Percent Low Income	−0.2931	−0.3778	1.29
	Percent Black	−0.2307	−0.2198	0.95
	Percent Latino	−0.1146	−0.0683	0.60
Financial	Instruction Funds	0.3530	4.3350	NA
	Teacher Salaries	1.2444	0.8696	0.70
	Percent State Aid	0.0303	0.0601	1.98
Policy	Attendance	0.9187	0.7616	0.83
	Gifted Classes	0.1985	0.1297	0.65
	Class Size	−0.9083	−1.1558	1.27
Teachers	Noncertified	−0.1256	−0.1643	1.31
	Teacher Experience	−0.0006	0.0598	N/A

regressions. In addition to the striking findings in Figure 5.1, there are a variety of incremental differences between the sets of agencies.

All other things being equal, the coefficients for the above average agencies are 29% larger for low-income students, 5 percent smaller for black students, and a fairly dramatic 40% smaller for Latino students.[5] The coefficient for teachers' salaries is 30% smaller in the pretty good districts, suggesting that salaries per se are not as important in these districts; at the same time, instructional funds (now 95% CI bounded away from zero) and state aid (+98%) are far more important.[6] The relationship for teacher certification is 31% larger for the pretty good districts. In terms of policies, the pretty good agencies have a 35% smaller relationship for gifted classes, 17% smaller for attendance, and 27% larger for class size.

5.5 The Super Agencies

Although the contrast between the average districts and the pretty good agencies is worth an extended discussion, we have already done that in Chapter 4. Our interest

---

[5]Substantively, this means the pretty good agencies are more affected by low-income students but less affected by minority students. More directly stated, minority students' pass rates are higher in the pretty good districts.

[6]Why might state aid be so important to these school districts? In organizational terms, one needs to remember that major state aid for education is a relatively recent phenomenon in Texas. Many school districts are like organizations that have been on severe financial diets for many years. The best of these organizations have lots of ideas for improvement but lack the money necessary to implement them. State aid essentially provides new monies and taps this reservoir of built-up reforms.

here is the excellent agencies, those that do a great deal better than even the pretty good agencies. To provide leverage on this problem, we essentially repeated the above analysis but changed the selection criterion from 0.7 to 0.8. We continued this approach by increasing the jackknifed residual selection parameter by 0.1 eight additional times until the last SWLS regression procedure used a jackknifed residual of 1.6.

Table 5.4 shows how this process focused on fewer and fewer agencies that performed better and better by providing the means and standard deviations of the increasingly select group of unweighted cases. The barchart shows the numbers of remaining cases as heights of the bars with the associated mean value written above each. The pretty good regression, as noted above, was not all that selective, with some 123 of 534 districts qualifying. The pretty good districts still had a significantly higher mean pass rate (65.0) than did all districts (55.6). The number of districts in the elite category continues to drop as the jackknifed residual increases to 1.6 until only 21 agencies, less than 4 percent of the total, remain in the high-performing category. These 21 agencies have an average pass rate of 73.8, well earning their "supermarket" designation. Table 5.4 does not show the exact difference between the pretty good agencies and the super agencies. Using a regression with dummy explanatory variables for jackknifed residuals greater than 0.7 and for those greater than 1.6 shows that pretty good agencies outperform the "other agencies" by 10.5 percentage points. The supermarkets, in turn, outperform the pretty good agencies by an additional 10.6 percentage points.

5.6 Lucky or Good?

A key theoretical question concerning the difference between the super agencies and the pretty good agencies is, are they actually better or just lucky? One view of quality versus luck is to determine whether the super agencies have more favorable environments than the other agencies. If the super agencies have more favorable inputs, then the argument that they are lucky rather than good gains some credence. If the inputs are relatively equal, then the difference is in what the agencies do with their inputs. Translating inputs into higher levels of outputs requires some skill rather than just luck.[7]

---

[7]We are overstating the case somewhat. That is, an agency could try something and get better performance by some quirk of fate. The true test distinguishing between those agencies that are lucky and those that are good requires a longer-term assessment. An agency that outperforms its peers with the same inputs year after year cannot be tagged with the term "lucky."

5 *Separating Excellent Agencies from the Good Ones: Extremes of the Data Distribution* **91**

Table 5.4 Number of Agencies and Average Pass Rate

Jackknifed Residual	N	Mean	Standard Deviation
0.7	123	65.0	10.1
0.8	112	65.6	9.9
0.9	93	66.4	9.5
1.0	73	67.1	10.0
1.1	59	70.7	9.0
1.2	50	68.3	9.2
1.3	39	69.6	9.7
1.4	34	70.8	9.5
1.5	24	73.9	6.7
1.6	21	73.8	6.8

Table 5.5 compares the means for the explanatory variables for the super agencies and the other agencies. Despite the 19-point difference in pass rates, the means of the explanatory variables are relatively similar. In only two cases are the mean differences for explanatory variables 95% CI bounded away from zero—class size and per capita instructional funds. The super agencies have a mean class size of 14.2 (compared to 15.4) and spend $165 more in instructional monies per pupil. These are relatively modest differences and can account for no more than two percentage points of the 19-percentage-point difference in pass rates

Table 5.5 Super Agencies and the Also-Rans: A Comparison

		Mean Values		95% CI	
	Explanatory Variable	Super Agencies	Others		
Environment	Percent Low Income	39.6	40.6	[6.84:	−8.84]
	Percent Black	9.3	11.5	[3.40:	−7.80]
	Percent Latino	28.8	31.2	[9.98:	−14.78]
Financial	Instruction Funds	2411.5	2246.7	[1.66:	327.94]
	Teacher Salaries	25,785.1	25,878.0	[665.78:	−851.58]
	Percent State Aid	47.8	48.0	[7.64:	−8.04]
Policy	Attendance	96.0	96.1	[0.38:	−0.58]
	Gifted Classes	6.4	6.7	[1.13:	−1.73]
	Class Size	14.2	15.4	[−0.44:	−1.96]
Teachers	Noncertified	5.3	5.2	[−1.30:	1.50]
	Experience	12.1	11.4	[−0.05:	1.45]
Outcome Variable	Pass Rate	73.8	54.8	[14.43:	23.57]

between the two groups from the models. Kaufman's theory that organizations survive because they are lucky does not appear to hold for these agencies. The super agencies differ from the average agency, not because the super agencies are lucky but rather because they are better at turning their relatively scarce inputs into valued outputs.

5.7 What the Super Agencies Do Differently

Table 5.6 presents the final SWLS results for the exceptional agencies regression ($R_j > +1.6$). The slopes in this regression are compared in relative terms to those for all agencies and those for the pretty good agency regression in Table 5.7 and in Figure 5.2. Table 5.6 suggests that the excellent agencies are affected by far fewer forces in their environment. The coefficient estimate for Latino students no longer has a 95% CI bounded away from zero—a striking result suggesting that perhaps in these districts Latino students do about as well on the achievement test as Anglo students.[8] Two other variables that are 95% CI bounded away from zero for both

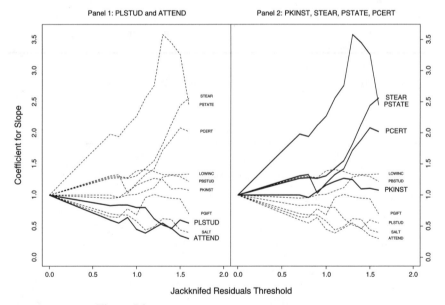

Figure 5.2 SWLS, Slope Changes for Excellent Analysis

---

[8] In substantive terms, this remarkable finding suggests that the super districts have found a way to achieve equity in test scores between Anglos and Latinos. Exactly what the districts are doing needs to be probed via a series of in-depth case studies. Note that this result, precisely stated, means that

Table 5.6 The Excellent Agencies

	Outcome Variable = Exam Pass Rates			
	Explanatory Variable	Slope	Std. Error	95% CI
	Intercept	61.0073	25.9944	[10.0583: 111.9563]
Environment	Percent Low Income	−0.3916	0.0525	[−0.4945: −0.2887]
	Percent Black	−0.2814	0.0479	[−0.3753: −0.1875]
	Percent Latino	−0.0632	0.0366	[−0.1349: 0.0085]
Financial	Instruction Funds	4.6992†	2.3335	[0.1255: 9.2729]
	Teacher Salaries	0.4992†	0.4729	[−0.4277: 1.4261]
	Percent State Aid	0.0766	0.0291	[0.0196: 0.1336]
Policy	Attendance	0.2760	0.2423	[−0.1989: 0.7509]
	Gifted Classes	0.1392	0.1444	[−0.1438: 0.4222]
	Class Size	−2.3293	0.4591	[−3.2291: −1.4295]
Teachers	Noncertified	−0.2533	0.0833	[−0.4166: −0.0900]
	Experience	0.3409	0.3034	[−0.2538: 0.9356]

†Explanatory variable in thousands of dollars
Multiple $R^2 = 0.49$
$F = 45.82$ on 11 and 522 degrees of freedom
Residual Standard Error = 2.793 on 522 degrees of freedom

Table 5.7 The Excellent Agencies and the Pretty Good Agencies

		Ratio of Excellent Slope to:	
	Explanatory Variable	All Agencies	Pretty Good Slope
Environment	Percent Low Income	1.34	1.04
	Percent Black	1.22	1.28
	Percent Latino	0.55	0.92
Financial	Instruction Funds	†	1.08
	Teacher Salaries	0.40	0.57
	Percent State Aid	2.52	1.27
Policy	Attendance	0.30	0.36
	Gifted Classes	0.70	1.08
	Class Size	2.56	2.02
Teachers	Noncertified	2.02	1.54

†Variable not distinct from zero in OLS equation

94   Jeff Gill, Kenneth J. Meier

all districts and the pretty good regression—attendance and teacher salaries—also drop to a 95% CI covering zero. The very best districts do not appear restricted by either their absenteeism rate or the inability to pay higher salaries (note from Table 5.5 that teacher salaries do not statistically differ between these two groups). The super district regression also repeats the pattern of the pretty good regression that gifted classes do not matter.

For three variables, the relationships for excellent agencies look fairly similar to those for the pretty good districts: low-income students, black students, and instructional funding. In the latter case, both the pretty good and the excellent regressions show a significant relationship, but the all agencies regression does not. What distinguishes the excellent from the pretty good regression are the other three relationships: class size, teacher certification, and state aid. Excellent districts get twice the impact of reducing class size as the pretty good districts get. Excellent districts also get about 54% more from better teacher qualifications and 27% more from increases in state aid. If one were to focus on a single variable that appears to distinguish the excellent districts from the pretty good ones, it would be in what these districts do as they reduce the size of their classes.

Given the cogent summary that the final regressions provide of the difference between excellent and pretty good agencies, one might ask was it worthwhile going through the iterative process? Why not simply jump to the final results (assuming that one would not jump too far and not have any districts remaining)? The iterative process contains a great deal of useful information, as illustrated in Figure 5.2, Panel 1. This panel charts the change in slopes for percent Latino students and attendance as the weights change with the other explanatory variables in the background. For Latino students, there is a gap between all districts and the pretty good districts. Even though the excellent districts' slope for Latinos is not 95% CI bounded away from zero and the pretty good slope is 95% CI bounded away from zero, in substantive terms they are about the same size. The gains achieved by the excellent districts, therefore, are already apparent in the pretty good districts. A different pattern is shown for attendance. Pretty good districts do not overcome attendance problems with nearly the skill that excellent districts do. Not until the jackknifed residual is set at 1.0 does the slope begin to drop, and it drops at a linear rate from that point onward.

Figure 5.2, Panel 2, highlights changes in slopes for instructional funding, certification, class size, and state aid with the other explanatory variables in the background. Instructional funding in Figure 5.2 shows a major jump from all districts (where it has a 95% CI covering zero) to the pretty good districts. Excellent districts really do not get much more out of additional instructional funds than the pretty good districts do, suggesting that the process for doing so is fairly

---

there is no statistical evidence of a difference in test scores between Latino and non-Latino students, given these data and this model.

well known to districts with above average talents. Certification and class size form a different pattern with excellent districts doing much better than the pretty good ones. The real differences appear at jackknifed residuals of +1.0 and higher, suggesting that a fairly high level of skills is needed to maximize return from such resources. Finally, Figure 5.2 also indicates that the state aid curve has eventually diminishing marginal return. The impact of state aid, while higher among the excellent agencies than the pretty good ones, actually peaks at a jackknifed residual of 1.3. So although there appear to be major initial gains that a state could make by having an aid system that discriminated by how well a school district used the aid, the number of affected districts should be larger rather than smaller.

Another interesting way to look at the effects of progressive weighting is to plot the slope changes for each type of agency (pretty good and super) as the weighting progresses; see Figure 5.3. The top panel shows these changes for SWAT with a jackknifed residual threshold of 0.7, and the bottom panel shows these changes for SWAT with a jackknifed residual threshold of 1.6. The top panel with the pretty good districts shows a less dramatic spreading of the slopes than the bottom panel with the super cases.

Looking at the bottom panel for super cases, we can notice immediately that the variable for percent of funds used for instructional purposes dramatically rises as

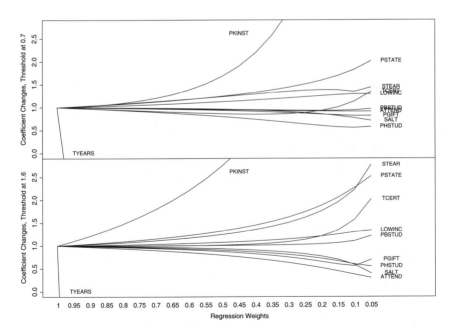

Figure 5.3 SWLS, Slope Changes as Weights Decline

96   *Jeff Gill, Kenneth J. Meier*

the weights decline, which implies that this variable is increasingly important for high-performing districts. However, this variable does not have a coefficient with 95% confidence interval bounded away from zero in the OLS model. Conversely, the variable indicating student teacher ratio (STEAR) climbs dramatically and has an OLS coefficient with a 95% confidence interval bounded away from zero. Recall that the OLS coefficient is negative so the dramatic increase is really a dramatic increase in the negative direction. This observation makes intuitive sense because it is generally known that larger class sizes provide poorer learning environments.

The slopes for explanatory variables for percent low income and percent black change very little as the weights are adjusted, which implies that these explanations do not affect high-performing cases substantively differently than typical cases. Note also that both of these variables had OLS coefficients with 95% confidence intervals bounded away from zero.

5.8 Extensions

This chapter uses SWAT to distinguish between public agencies that are "pretty good" at their job and those that are excellent. The process uses a SWAT technique to alter the focus to progressively better performance, and can be used in a wide variety of public policy and public management situations.

First, although the focus here was on the best performers, quite clearly the emphasis could also be on the worst performers (see Chapter 4). An interesting situation might be one in which public agencies are interested in preventing the worst-case scenario. In environmental protection, for example, the nature of risk assessment is such that policy makers are concerned with what the most extreme cases could be. If adequate models of environmental quality can be constructed, then SWAT techniques can focus on environmental cases with negative residuals and with those further and further below the regression line.

Second, the process can also be used to study regulatory compliance. In all areas of regulation, some firms comply rather quickly with the law. Others are more reticent and some resist compliance with every resource at their possession. With a measure of compliance, SWAT can be used to construct models of the most resistant to compliance (all other things being equal) and to focus on how those firms make decisions different from the average firm.[9]

Third, additional work should focus on the situation where the number of "exceptional" cases becomes too small to provide any meaningful information. Quite clearly the selection criterion can be increased and fewer and fewer programs will qualify. The benefit of fewer programs is that those selected are more likely

---

[9]The method likely has some application in the area of deviant behavior. Because our concerns are with how organizations deal with their environments, we leave these issues for others to address.

to be the elite programs. The disadvantage is that there might be so few of these programs that their activities and processes cannot be generalized (or serve as role models) to other public organizations.

Fourth, SWAT techniques are clearly applicable to a wide variety of private-sector activities. In any situation where goals are relatively clear and a production function can be set up, the technique can provide a wealth of useful information. Nothing in the public-private distinction prevents the application of this technique in the private sector.

5.9 Discussion

We make two distinct points in this chapter. First, bureaucracies are heterogeneous, highly differentiated creatures. Yet, many perceive a unitary, monolithic structure without substantive differences in competencies. A partial cause is a traditional focus on the average case as the unit of analysis (Goodsell 1983). Another contributing causal factor is a uniform and negative view held by the general public. Politicians, mostly on the right-hand side of the spectrum, often run *against* federal and state bureaucracies (a second rate actor from California being the best example). We show that superior and vastly superior bureaucracies use their resources in fundamentally different ways. The distinction is important because it demonstrates that uniform and simplistic prescriptive advice (Osborne and Gaebler 1992) is unlikely to produce effective results for all possible applications.

Second, the qualitative SWAT technique can be exploited to highlight differences between the merely good performers and the truly stellar performers. What we can learn from each group is fundamentally different. The super agencies are distinguished by their ability to turn necessarily limited resources into measurable output in a superior fashion. The super agencies do not have more resources than the other agencies. They achieve success by using a mix of resources available to others, but in an optimal manner. In particular, superior agencies are more in control of their destiny: they were found to be less affected by environmental variables not easily manipulated (demographic student measures). Here the SWAT technique focuses not just on who the stellar performers are, but on how they achieved that status. We can think of no better prescriptive advice for public managers.

5.10 References

Burtless, Gary. 1996. *Does Money Matter? The Effect of School Resources on Student Achievement and Adult Success.* Washington, D.C.: Brookings Institution.

Chubb, John, and Terry Moe. 1989. *Politics, Markets and America's Schools.* Washington, D.C.: Brookings Institution.

Downs, Anthony. 1967. *Inside Bureaucracy.* Boston: Little, Brown.

Goodsell, Charles T. 1983. *The Case for Bureaucracy.* Chatham, NJ: Chatham House.

Hanushek, Eric A. 1996. "School Resources and Student Performance." In *Does Money Matter? The Effect of School Resources on Student Achievement and Adult Success,* edited by Gary Burtless. Washington, D.C.: Brookings Institution.

Hanushek, Eric A. 1989. "The Impact of Differential Expenditures on School Performance." *Educational Researcher* 23: 45–65.

Hanushek, Eric A. 1986. "The Economics of Schooling: Production and Efficiency in Public Schools." *Journal of Economic Literature* 24: 1141–77.

Kaufman, Herbert. 1991. *Time, Chance and Organizations: Natural Selection in a Perilous Environment.* Washington, D.C.: Brookings Institution.

Lan, Zhiyong, and David H. Rosenbloom. 1992. "Public Administration in Transition?" (Editorial) *Public Administration Review* 52: 535–7.

Leamer, Edward E. 1978. *Specification Searches: Ad Hoc Inference with Nonexperimental Data.* New York: Wiley.

Meier, Kenneth J. 1993. *Politics and the Bureaucracy.* Pacific Grove, CA: Brooks/Cole.

Osborne, David, and Ted Gaebler. 1992. *Re-Inventing Government: How the Entrepreeurial Spirit Is Transforming the Public Sector.* Reading, MA: Addison-Wesley.

Poveda, Tony G. 1990. *Lawlessness and Reform: The FBI in Transition.* Pacific Grove, CA: Brooks/Cole.

Rourke, Francis. 1984. *Bureaucracy, Politics and Public Policy.* Third edition. Boston: Little Brown.

Simon, Herbert. 1947. *Administrative Behavior.* New York: Free Press.

Smith, Kevin B. 1995. "Policy, Markets, and Bureaucracy: Reexamining School Choice." *Journal of Politics* 56: 475–491.

Thompson, James D. 1967. *Organizations in Action.* New York: McGraw-Hill.

Wolf, Patrick. 1997. "Why Must We Reinvent the Federal Government? Putting Historical Developmental Claims to the Test." *Journal of Public Administration Research and Theory* 7: 353–89.

Chapter 6

Weighting with an Exogenous Variable or with Two Exogenous Variables: Equity Versus Excellence in Organizations[1]

Kenneth J. Meier, Jeff Gill, Robert D. Wrinkle, J. L. Polinard

6.1 Introduction

Previous chapters have considered a variety of goals for agencies and programs. In each case, however, only one goal was considered at a time, and the goals (effectiveness, risk aversion, etc.) were derived by making weighted case level changes based on jackknifed residuals. This chapter uses substantively weighted analytical techniques (SWAT) to develop an approach incorporating two or more goals. In the first developed example, one of these goals, effectiveness, will be the

---

[1]Portions of this chapter were presented at the annual meeting of the Midwest Political Science Association, Chicago, IL, April 1997. A revised version of that paper appeared in the *American Review of Public Administration* 29 (March 1999), 5–18.

outcome variable; the other, equity, will be incorporated as an exogenous factor. In a second example, we will provide a general way to deal with multiple goals and then use both equity and effectiveness as weight variables. As long as at most one goal is endogenous, two or more goals can be used to structure the SWAT analysis.

6.2 The Theoretical Setting for the Study

According to Okun (1976), the great trade-off in public policy is between equity and efficiency.[2] That statement is accepted as a truism about organizations also; any organization with multiple goals (such as both equity and excellence) will by definition have some measure of goal conflict and therefore some confusion in the organization (Downs 1967; Rainey 1997, p. 14, Simon 1957, pp .176, 178; Goodsell 1989, p. 518). The perception is that organizations can be equitable or they can be efficient/effective but not both (Rainey 1997, p. 73); much of the challenge of the New Public Administration was that bureaucracies sought efficiency without any concerns about social equity (Waldo 1971; Frederickson 1997).[3] At the same time, little empirical scholarship exists on this issue; and the question could be addressed empirically if good measures of equity and excellence were available. For these reasons, public school systems form an ideal setting for examining how organizations deal with demands for equity and efficiency.

School systems are no different from other complex organizations in their approach to goals and goal conflict. Historically, the U.S. education system has often emphasized excellence for the few at the expense of equity for others (Tyack 1974; Oakes 1985). Through organizational policies of ability grouping and tracking, selective enforcement of truancy and dropout laws, and selective counseling, school systems can provide a two-tiered educational system that provides excellent college preparatory education for white middle-class students and at the same time funnels the poor, immigrants, and minorities into vocational and general education. Lipsky (1980) calls this behavior "skimming," meaning that administrators skim off a small percentage of recipients for special service. The idea is that scarce resources are directed towards the cases that can get the most out of them. Obviously this is the worst-case scenario in terms of equity, particularly when the decision criteria involve race.

---

[2]This chapter uses the terms *effective* and *efficient* as interchangeable. As Simon (1957, p. 188) notes, "The problem of efficiency is to find the maximum production function, with the constraint that total expenditure is fixed." Thus effectiveness and efficiency converge given a specified level of resources and agreement on what an organization produces.

[3]The urban services literature deals somewhat indirectly with this issue. See the summary of that literature in Frederickson (1997).

The historical trade-of between equity and excellence raises a serious concern about the more recent educational reforms of the 1980s and 1990s (see Garaway 1995; Murphy 1989). These reforms, however, took place in an environment much different from that of the "one best system" reforms of the early twentieth century (Anyon 1995; Katz 1992). Advocates of equity abound, and minorities have used their access to the political system to pressure school systems to pay attention to equity concerns (Polinard et al. 1994; Meier and Stewart 1991). Contemporary school systems, therefore, face demands for both equity and excellence.

Faced with two sets of demands, how would a rational organization respond? Public organizations are no strangers to multiple goals (Rainey 1997, p. 128). One logical response would be to break down the multiple goals into their component problems (Perrow 1970, p. 173), reorganize the agency (Thompson 1967, p. 79), and design processes to address the problems separately (Simon 1957, p. 191). Alternatively, the organization might try several different experimental processes to learn how to meet the multiple goals (Downs 1967, p. 224). As long as the goals are not diametrically opposed to each other, the organization can then integrate these individual processes to generate satisfactory results. The entire process is likely to be iterative as the organization incrementally determines how much real conflict exists between the goals in practice and with varying types of technology. Although meeting multiple goals is more difficult than meeting a single goal (Katz and Kahn 1966, p. 266), it is not impossible.

Within an organization, therefore, whether or not equity must be traded off for excellence is an open question (Murphy 1989). This chapter illustrates the linkage between equity and excellence by using the SWAT technique substantively weighted least squares (SWLS), but could also have been performed with generalized substantively reweighted least squares (GSRLS) if there had been a motivation for a different jackknifed residuals threshold.

First, a model of educational performance using a set of Texas school districts will be constructed. Within that model, measures of excellence and equity will be created. Second, the logic of SWAT will be modified so that it can assess organizational performance subject to the constraint of equity. Third, results from the analysis will demonstrate that (a) achieving equity, far from being detrimental to excellence, may actually be a complement, and (b) organizations that achieve excellence in the context of equity are subtly different from those that do not. Fourth, we will then generalize the technique with a second example.

6.3 Educational Performance

The dataset used in this analysis contains 527 Texas school districts with at least 500 students and no more than 90 percent Anglo students. In addition, to make sure the districts are comparable, each district must operate at least one high school to be included in the universe.[4] All data are from the 1991 school year and were provided by the Texas Education Agency.

6.3.1 The Outcome Variable

The state of Texas requires all students to take standardized competency tests in the third, fifth, seventh, ninth, and eleventh grades. The outcome variable, our measure of excellence, is simply the percentage of students who passed this exam in 1991. The mean pass rate was 55.9 percent with a standard deviation of 10.8. The mean scores are approximately normally distributed (Figure 6.1), and range from a low of 26.6 percent to a high of 91.4 percent. Checking this assumption is an important step in SWAT analysis (Chapter 3).

Our equity measure, Q, is also based on these test scores. It is the proportion of black and Latino students who pass the test divided by the proportion of Anglo students who pass the test:

$$Q = \frac{P_{\text{black/Latino}}}{P_{\text{Anglo}}} \qquad (6.1)$$

As this measure approaches 1.0, it means that minority students are performing on a par with Anglo students. The mean of the equity measure is 0.61 with a

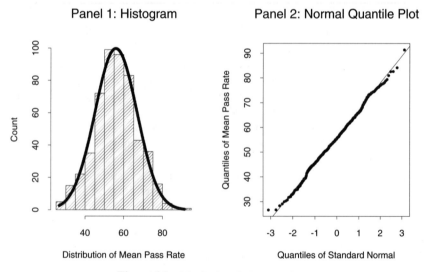

Figure 6.1 Distribution of Mean Pass Rate

---

[4]This restriction makes this dataset slightly different from that used in Chapter 4. A small number of districts in that sample did not maintain a high school.

standard deviation of 0.12. The districts range from a low of 0.29 on the equity scale (a minority student is 71% less likely to pass the exam than an Anglo student) to a high of 1.08 (a minority student is 8% more likely to pass the exam). The measure has a slight right-hand-side skew (Figure 6.2). The correlation between the excellence measure and the equity measure is 0.32, suggesting that equity need not be sacrificed for high performance on the exam.

6.3.2 Explanatory Variables

The input-output analysis in organization studies is widely implemented in education policy with an education production function (Burtless 1996).[5] As noted in the previous chapter, organization performance should be a function of environmental constraints, resources applied to the process, and organization policies designed to improve performance. All performance models of public bureaucracy need to control for the types of input the bureaucracy receives.

The control variables for this model are: the percent eligible for free or reduced-price school lunches, per-pupil expenditures for instruction, the average teacher salary, the percentage of money from state funds, the average percentage of students who attend school, class size, gifted classes, teacher experience and certification, and the percentage of teachers who are minorities.

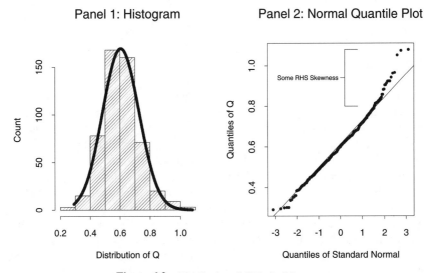

Figure 6.2 Distribution of Q Equity Measure

---
[5]This literature is far too large to cite comprehensively. See the extended bibliography in Burtless (1996).

6.4 Substantively Weighted Least Squares

In a typical SWLS analysis, we would run the above education production function and then use jackknifed residuals to weight a set of regressions to determine how effective districts differ from other districts (for example, see Chapter 4). Rather than focus on the high-performing school districts per se, our interest is on those school districts that get equitable results and at the same time still perform at a high level. That is, we seek to avoid those districts that actually trade-off equity and excellence. To do so, we follow an analogous strategy to that of Chapter 2. Based on our equity measure, we select the districts with approximately the highest 10 percent of equity scores (scores above 0.755, $n = 55$). We then run a series of regressions, all weighting the equity districts as equal to 1.0 and gradually reducing the weights of the other districts by 0.1 and finally to 0.05. By examining how the slopes change as these regressions are run, we can get indications of what the equitable districts are doing that is different from what the other districts are doing.

The basic philosophy underlying SWAT is that organizations differ in their ability to transform inputs into outputs. The analyst needs to look at these differences to see what might be possible as a management reform. Such a philosophy is appropriate in this case because the consistent finding in the literature is that schools vary in quality and their ability to translate inputs into outputs. Money matters, the argument goes, but only in those schools that know how to use it (Hanushek 1996).

6.5 Findings

The first step in the SWLS process is to compare the two sets of programs—in this case, the equity programs and the nonequity programs. The means for each of the explanatory variables are shown in Table 6.1 along with the 95% confidence interval (CI) for the difference of means. There are four mean differences whose 95% confidence intervals are bounded away from zero (i.e., they have p-values of less than 0.05): percent low income, instructional money, class size, and minority staff. Equity districts spend about $300 more per pupil on instruction, have slightly smaller class sizes, but get less of their money from the state. These are not major differences, especially with over 500 cases. There are also two additional (but without mean difference 95% confidence intervals bounded away from zero) factors that might disadvantage the equity programs–a slightly larger proportion of uncertified teachers, and slightly less experienced teachers.

To investigate these four mean differences that are 95% CI bounded away from zero, we create a spread versus level plot for each in Figure 6.3. Spread vs level plots simultaneously provide a measure of central tendency for grouped data (jittered median) and a measure of dispersion (median absolute deviation or

Table 6.1 Comparing Equity Districts with Other Districts

		District Mean Values		Mean Difference:
	Explanatory Variable	Equity	Other	95% CI
Environment	Percent Low Income	35.4	40.4	[−9.8152: −0.3474]
Financial	Instructional Money (K)	2.5	2.2	[0.0908: 0.4436]
	Teacher Salaries (K)	26.1	25.9	[−0.4059: 0.8404]
	State Aid Percent	43.2	48.3	[−11.1542: 1.0778]
Policy	Attendance	96.1	96.0	[−0.3662: 0.5596]
	Gifted Classes	6.9	6.6	[−0.4618: 1.0773]
	Class Size	14.3	15.4	[−1.6429: −0.5628]
Teachers	Minority Staff	16.7	24.1	[−13.5810: −1.4065]
	Certified Teachers	6.0	5.0	[−0.5970: 2.6351]
	Teacher Experience	11.1	11.5	[−0.9153: 0.0703]

MAD). When groups are closer on the x-axis, it means that although the difference was 95% CI bounded away from zero, the effect size is nonetheless small. Groups that are more dispersed on the y-axis are more spread out from the group median. Lines connect the median value on the x-axis with the median of the MADs. Jittering adds a small amount of imprecision distributed normally with mean zero

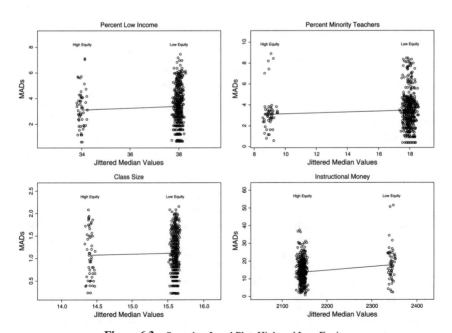

Figure 6.3 Spread vs Level Plot, High and Low Equity

106   Kenneth J. Meier, Jeff Gill, Robert D. Wrinkle, J. L. Polinard

in order to spread out points on top of each other or nearly on top of each other in the display.

Some interesting findings are apparent from Figure 6.3. It appears that a small number (five) of the high-equity districts have very dissimilar approaches to the hiring of minority teachers from other high-equity districts. This observation could perhaps be motivation to look at theses cases in detail, from either a policy or legal perspective. In addition, there is graphical evidence of the important difference in how the two types of districts handle instructional money.

The second step in the SWLS process is to run an ordinary least squares (OLS) regression; the results are shown in Table 6.2. Since these results provide a base from which to compare, some discussion is in order. Before discussing these results, however, we need to look at the scatterplot of predicted versus actual results in Figure 6.4. The pattern does not resemble any of the problematic ones that we identified in Chapter 1, so SWAT appears to be appropriate.

Also of concern is whether or not sufficient variation remains to allow SWAT techniques to work. The scatterplot appears to show good variation around the fit, and the standard error of the regression is a healthy 7.33 percentage points. Going two standard errors in either direction suggests a range of approximately 29 percentage points, which is well worth examining in terms of student performance.

In terms of the specific linear model coefficients, environmental constraints have a major impact on student performance. For every 1 percentage point increase of students from low-income families, the exam pass rate drops by 0.34 percentage

Table 6.2   Linear Model, Educational Excellence: Determinants of Pass Rates

	Outcome Variable = Exam Pass Rates			
	Explanatory Variable	Coefficient	Std. Error	95% CI
	Intercept	−53.1971	29.4513	[−110.9215: 4.5273]
Environment	Percent Low Income	−0.3362	0.0311	[−0.3972:−0.2752]
Financial	Instructional Money (K)	0.1319	1.8389	[−3.4723: 3.7361]
	Teacher Salaries (K)	1.4764	0.3623	[0.7663: 2.1865]
	State Aid Percent	0.0394	0.0254	[−0.0104: 0.0892]
Policy	Attendance	1.0516	0.2993	[0.4648: 1.6384]
	Gifted Classes	0.1836	0.1030	[−0.0183: 0.3855]
	Class Size	−0.9252	0.3513	[−1.6137:−0.2367]
Teachers	Minority Staff	−0.1054	0.0249	[−0.1540:−0.0568]
	Certified Teachers	−0.0875	0.0731	[−0.2308: 0.0558]
	Teacher Experience	−0.2660	0.2254	[−0.7078: 0.1758]

Adjusted $R^2 = 0.55$
$F = 22.37849$ on 10 and 516 degrees of freedom
Residual Standard Error = 7.33 on 516 degrees of freedom

6   *Equity Versus Excellence in Organizations*   107

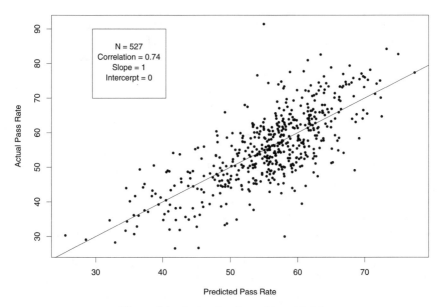

Figure 6.4   Student Pass Rates, Linear Model

point (all other things being equal). Second, money appears to matter but not in all cases. An increase of $1000 in teacher salaries is associated with an increase of 1.48 percentage points of students who pass the exam. Neither per capita instructional funds nor percentage of state funds, however, has a coefficient estimate 95% CI bounded away from zero.

The three non-teacher policies are all related to student performance in the predicted directions, but one (gifted classes) does not have a 95% confidence interval bounded away from zero. An increase of 1 percentage point increase in student attendance is associated with a 1.05 percentage point increase in student performance. In addition, an increase in class size of one student per teacher is associated with a drop of 0.93 percentage point in student performance.

Teacher policy measures are not positively related to performance; in fact, all the coefficients are negative. Neither the relationship for noncertified teachers nor the relationship for teacher experience has a coefficient estimate 95% CI bounded away from zero. The minority staff percentage does, suggesting that for every percentage point increase in minority staff, student performance drops by 0.1 percentage point. This finding is a direct challenge to the literature that contends minority teachers benefit minority students. These results suggest that any minority student benefit from minority teachers might be at the expense of nonminority students since the slope coefficient is negative.

Ten iterations of SWLS were run on this regression using the equity measure to select weights for the weighted least squares. Each regression decreased the weight for the low-equity cases by 0.1 except the last run, which used 0.05 (so that the last weight was 0.05). To illustrate how the regression coefficients change, we present the slope change graphs in Figure 6.5. In both panels, the metric treats the OLS coefficients in Table 6.2 as equal to 1.0 so that graphs can be interpreted as proportional changes in the slopes.

Figure 6.5, Panel 1, shows the values of the slopes for the state aid percentage and teacher salaries as the low-equity districts receive less weight. The percentage of state aid, which is not 95% CI bounded away from zero in the ordinary least squares regression, gradually increases in impact until the slope is 2.16 times larger in the final weighted regression. Figure 6.5, Panel 1, also shows how the impact of teacher salaries decreases as the nonequity districts are downweighted until it is no longer 95% CI bounded away from zero (about 42% of the original impact).

Figure 6.5, Panel 2, illustrates the range of patterns with graphs for class size, gifted classes, class attendance, and percent minority staff. Gifted classes and attendance show only moderate changes. Class size increases in impact,

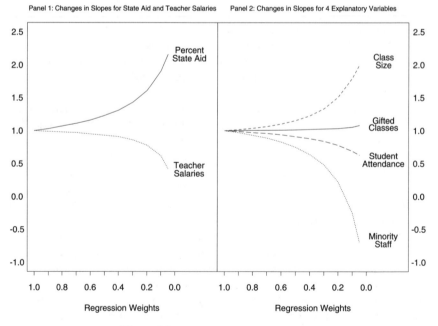

Figure 6.5 SWLS, Variable Slope Changes

eventually doubling the size of the slope coefficient. Percent minority staff has an especially interesting pattern. The percent minority staff was negatively related to student performance in the OLS equation. As the nonequity districts are downweighted, however, the negative impact of this variable drops eventually to nonsignificance (95% CI covering zero) and then becomes positive and significant (95% CI bounded away from zero). In districts with greater equity, percent minority staff is associated with increased student performance.

The final SWLS regression is shown in Table 6.3. An examination of the relationships shows that equitable districts have patterns distinctly different from those of nonequitable districts. An examination of these differences can provide clues as to factors that permit a school system to pursue both excellence and equity. These differences are also shown graphically in Figure 6.6, the multiregression barplot.

In equitable districts, the constraint of the economic environment is greater; the impact of low-income students is 61 percent greater in the equity districts. This does not mean that equity districts, as a result, generate lower performance; their mean pass rate is 64 percent compared to 55 percent for the nonequity districts. The relationship likely signifies that equity districts have overcome some of the poverty factors and are now faced with the most hard-core cases, thus the greater level of constraint.

Table 6.3   SWLS, Excellence Constrained by Equity: Determinants of Pass Rate

	Outcome Variable = Exam Pass Rates			
	Explanatory Variable	Coefficient	Std. Error	95% CI
	Intercept	15.7082	24.811	[−32.9214: 64.3378]
Environment	Percent Low Income	−0.5427	0.0362	[−0.6137:−0.4717]
Financial	Instructional Money (K)	2.7821	1.5950	[−0.3441: 5.9083]
	Teacher Salaries (K)	0.6269	0.4129	[−0.1824: 1.4362]
	State Aid Percent	0.0852	0.0275	[0.0313: 0.1391]
Policy	Attendance	0.6652	0.2599	[0.1558: 1.1746]
	Gifted Classes	0.1985	0.1351	[−0.0663: 0.4633]
	Class Size	−1.8488	0.3484	[−2.5317:−1.1659]
Teachers	Minority Staff	0.0730	0.0267	[0.0207: 0.1253]
	Certified Teachers	−0.2034	0.0764	[−0.3531:−0.0537]
	Teacher Experience	0.0271	0.2666	[−0.4954: 0.5496]

Weighting: $\beta = 0.05$
Adjusted $R^2 = 0.51$
$F = 18.1391$ on 10 and 516 degrees of freedom
Residual Standard Error = 3.30 on 516 degrees of freedom

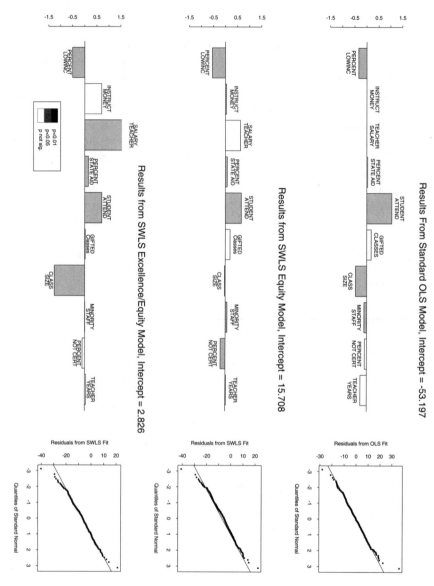

Figure 6.6 Barplot for Texas Data

The financial variables indicate that state aid is a key for equitable districts. Each percentile increase in state aid has 2.16 times the impact in equity districts. Although Texas is not known as a state with major redistributive funding for education, what funding it does provide appears crucial for those districts concerned with equity.[6] Teacher salaries and per capita instructional funding are no longer 95% CI bounded away from zero although the teacher salaries coefficient was significantly nonzero in the linear model. This finding suggests that, unlike typical cases, money allocated to instructional programs and teacher salaries are not key organizational criteria in these equitable school systems.[7]

The policy variables show another divergent pattern. Class attendance is much less important in the equity districts than in all districts. It is still a positive factor, but at a much lower level (63%), suggesting that class attendance is only a necessary condition for learning. Once students are in class, performance depends on other factors. Expanded gifted classes seem to matter little in terms of the equity districts. What does matter a great deal is class size. A reduction in the size of classes has twice the impact in equity districts, which suggests that equity districts get more effective teaching out of smaller classes than do the nonequity districts.

Finally, teacher variables, with one exception, remain disappointing. The one exception is minority staff. In equity districts, percent minority staff is positively associated with higher performance; an increase of 1 percentage point in minority staff is associated with a 0.07 percentage point increase in pass rate. At this ratio, a 20 percentage point increase in minority staff has a modest 1.4 percentage point increase in pass rate. Given these are high-equity districts, it suggests that the impact of minority staff is in improving the performance of minority students, consistent with the work of Meier and Stewart (1992) and Polinard, Wrinkle, and Meier (1995). This finding is consistent with the suggestion by Hanushek (1989) that the highest priority in reform should be in improving the quality of staff. Clearly an interesting process analysis would focus on the role of minority staff in the equity districts relative to their role in nonequity districts. This finding also suggests that those who contend a representative bureaucracy might actually perform better could be correct (Thompson 1976).[8]

---

[6] From a management perspective, this result suggests looking at what equity districts do with state aid and how that differs from what the others do. This is an excellent situation for in-depth case studies.

[7] Some of this allocation might well be to technology, which blurs the distinction. In a study of statewide education systems, Waller (1997) found that technology (computer equipment, etc.) was significantly related to improvements in educational performance.

[8] This finding also suggests that a representative bureaucracy might also be valuable in the process of service delivery (see Theilemann and Stewart 1996).

6.6 Weighting in Two Dimensions

Although we have presented SWAT techniques that have weighted with only one variable, the techniques are clearly generalizable to more than one dimension as long as only one of the weights is endogenous to the model.[9] This section will briefly extend the example in this chapter to a two-dimensional problem.

Rather than a concern with equity or with performance subject to the constraint of equity, suppose the analyst is really interested in organizations that maximize both performance and equity at the same time. In general form, the SWAT approach to analysis is based on the following model:

$$\mathbf{Y} = \mathbf{X}_a \boldsymbol{\beta}_a + \boldsymbol{\omega}^{-1} \mathbf{X}_b \boldsymbol{\beta}_b \tag{6.2}$$

where

$\mathbf{Y}$ is the measure of output;
$\mathbf{X}_a$ is the design matrix containing the subset of programs of interest (e.g., high performers);
$\mathbf{X}_b$ is the design matrix containing the other programs;
$\boldsymbol{\beta}_a$ is the coefficient vector for the programs of interest;
$\boldsymbol{\beta}_b$ is the coefficient vector for the other programs;
$\boldsymbol{\omega}$ is a diagonal matrix containing the inverse of the substantive weights.

In this setup, the diagonal values in $\boldsymbol{\omega}$ are initially equal to 1.0, and the equation reduces to OLS regression. The $\boldsymbol{\omega}$ diagonals corresponding to cases that have jackknifed residuals below the designated threshold (0.7 in SWLS) are then gradually decreased, reducing the influence of the cases of less interest.

Whereas $\boldsymbol{\omega}$ has been defined as a weight vector that is based on values of the jackknifed residual (or in this chapter another variable):

$\boldsymbol{\omega} = f(\boldsymbol{\zeta})$, where $\boldsymbol{\zeta}$ is the vector of jackknifed residuals or some other desired exogenous variable.

---

[9]If both variables are endogenous, the analyst essentially must run two regressions to get two sets of jackknifed residuals. Unfortunately, our process outlined here does not solve the problem because after calculating the final weights, one still has two outcome variables. The solution, quite clearly, is a measurement one. The analyst must first combine the two outcome variables in some manner to get a single outcome variable. At that point, the SWAT process can be applied. If the performance dimensions cannot be combined for some reason, then one simply must run separate analyses. Our discussion here does not mean we favor reducing the dimensions of policy analysis; whether or not that is an acceptable procedure is context dependent.

Also ω could be defined as follows:

$\omega = f(\boldsymbol{\Xi})$, where $\boldsymbol{\Xi}$ is a matrix of k columns, each containing an additional variable.

At this point, the only problem is to determine how to combine the variables that make up $\boldsymbol{\Xi}$ so that a subset of programs can be designated as those of interest. The simplest method is to define a variable Ψ representing the Euclidean distance that the weight is from $\boldsymbol{\Xi}$:

$$\Psi = \|\boldsymbol{\omega} - \boldsymbol{\Xi}\|. \tag{6.3}$$

With this construct, the n-dimensional Euclidean norm, denoted by $\| \cdot \|$, allows more than two weight variables to be incorporated.

An important issue with this transformation is the included assumption that the two weight factors are of equal interest. Whether or not individual factors should be weighted equally depends on the context. This is a key decision that must be made by the analyst and openly acknowledged. If the decision is that some factors should play a greater role (e.g., that equity is twice as important as efficiency), then that decision needs to be made up front and defended; and the weight variable should be adjusted accordingly. The next section applies this setup to the running example.

6.7 Two-Dimensional Weights: An Illustration

Although equity and excellence were not opposed concepts in our Texas education example, neither were they strongly correlated ($r = 0.3216$). The analyst might be interested in programs that attain a high level of excellence and simultaneously a high level of performance.[10] In this case, we have two measures—a measure of equity (the ratio of minority pass rates to Anglo pass rates) and a measure of performance (the jackknifed residuals from the OLS regression). Since we are assuming that these criteria should be weighted equally, combining them is relatively simple.

First, the equity measure needs to be converted to a standardized measure by subtracting the mean from each score and dividing through by the standard deviation. Since jackknifed residuals are t-distributed, this transformation also gives the equity measure a corresponding zero mean and unity standard deviation.

---

[10] Any two criteria could be used in a dual-weight situation. The current example is somewhat artificial since we have already explored one dimension in context of another; but, as the example will illustrate, doing both at the same time is a somewhat different situation.

Second, because we are interested in programs that are high performers on both dimensions, a constant must be added to each variable to eliminate negative numbers.[11] In this case, the lowest value is approximately −4.2 for the jackknifed residuals, so 4.2 is added to both measures. For each program these two measures are squared, summed, and then a square root is taken to create our measure of Ψ, or the variable on which the weights will be based. Again we must decide the proportion of agencies to select into the top category. Let's simply take the top 10 percent of agencies or, in this case, those that score above 7.35 on the weight variable. Those above will be designated as the "equity/excellence" agencies and those below, the other agencies.

After this set of decisions, the process of SWLS continues as it has before. The other cases are downweighted in increments of 0.1 until the last regression contains a weight of 0.05. The final regression results are shown in Table 6.4 and may be viewed as the results for agencies that do well on both equity and performance simultaneously.

The multiregression barplot (Figure 6.6), comparing these results to the OLS results and the equity results, clearly indicates that the equity/excellence agencies are a fairly unique subset (at least in comparison to the equity districts). The examination of a few of the regression coefficients will demonstrate this.

Table 6.4   Student Test Scores Weighted by Both Equity and High Performance

Explanatory Variable		Outcome Variable = Exam Pass Rates		
		Coefficient	Std. Error	95% CI
	Intercept	2.8259	26.0871	[−48.304816: 53.956616]
Environment	Percent Low Income	−0.4985	0.0387	[−0.574352:−0.422648]
Financial	Instructional Money (K)	1.3991	1.7055	[−1.943680: 4.741880]
	Teacher Salaries (K)	1.7970	0.4385	[0.937540: 2.656460]
	State Aid Percent	0.1569	0.0270	[0.103980: 0.209820]
Policy	Attendance	0.7047	0.2566	[0.201764: 1.207636]
	Gifted Classes	0.0222	0.1306	[−0.233776: 0.278176]
	Class Size	−2.5380	0.3711	[−3.265356:−1.810644]
Teachers	Minority Staff	0.0104	0.0275	[−0.043500: 0.064300]
	Certified Teachers	−0.0997	0.0740	[−0.244740: 0.045340]
	Teacher Experience	0.0520	0.2670	[−0.471320: 0.575320]

Adjusted $R^2 = 0.51$
$F = 18.3383$ on 10 and 516 degrees of freedom
Residual Standard Error = 3.29 on 516 degrees of freedom

---

[11]If one were interested only in deviant programs, those very good or very bad, then a constant would not be necessary because the interest would be in distance from the origin, where the origin was set at the midpoints of the distributions.

The two relationships that differ the most from OLS are for state aid and student-teacher ratios. All other things being equal, an increase of 1 percentage point in state aid is associated with a 0.16 percentage point increase in test scores, a coefficient four times the size of the OLS coefficient and roughly double the coefficient for the equity districts. Similarly, an increase of one student per class is associated with a 2.5 percentage point drop in test scores, an impact 2.7 times the size of the OLS coefficient and about 30 percent larger than the equity coefficient. Consistent with the importance of money in these districts, the teacher salary relationship is positive and 95% CI bounded away from zero (unlike that for the equity districts).

Also of interest are the relationships that become insignificant (95% CI covering zero). For the equity and excellence districts, there is no evidence that teacher certification matters, and the slope for percent minority staff (negative in OLS and positive in equity districts) is effectively zero for these districts.

Even this brief recap of those districts that excel on both test scores and in terms of equity suggests that they are different from both the average group and those districts that stress equity. Doing two things well is obviously more difficult than doing one thing well. To be able to maximize two variables simultaneously requires an influx of money and the effective use of that money.

This two-variable example demonstrates that SWLS and SWAT techniques in general can be used with more than one criterion variable to select cases of interest. Although the presentation was limited to two variables, quite clearly the approach can be generalized to multiple variables. The only limits on the number of dimensions are substantive; that is, the final weight criterion should have some substantive meaning. As long as the analyst can describe in substantive terms how the selected subset of cases differs from the remainder of the cases, the number of variables used in the weighting processes is without limit. Establishing a composite variable as a weight, therefore, is essentially a measurement problem.

6.8 Discussion

This chapter illustrated the SWAT technique of substantively weighted least squares with an exogenous weight variable and extended the SWAT process to more than one weight variable. Because the substantive findings are also important to the policy literature, we summarize them here.

A long-standing concern in the policy literature is the tradeof between excellence (or efficiency) and equity (Okun 1976; Garaway 1995). This study challenges the tradeof viewpoint in two ways. First, there is not necessarily a tradeof between equity and excellence; some organizations can do both. Specifically, districts can perform well on the standard measures of educational performance without creating a tracked system that provides good-quality education to some students at the expense of others. The relationship between equity and excellence in these Texas districts was positive, not negative. Second, organizations that are equitable use their resources in ways different from those that are not. Money and class size matter more in these districts, suggesting that they use resources more effectively than the average system. The lesson is that organizations can attain multiple goals but must effectively use their resources to do so. Teacher salaries, experience, and certification matter less although percent minority staff becomes a positive factor.

These relationships suggest that how these districts organize their resources and their educational programs is what matters rather than the total amount of resources. Just as all organizations vary in their ability to transform inputs to outputs, school systems vary in their ability to take resources and produce educated students. Systems that stress equity are in general superior at this task to systems that do not.

A second example used two criteria for weights, both equity as exogenously defined and effectiveness as defined by the OLS jackknifed residual. This subset of districts was again different from both the OLS results and the equity districts. Money appeared to be the driving force, and these districts were able to use state aid, teacher salaries, and class size to obtain larger gains on student test scores.

Statistically, this chapter illustrates the flexibility of SWAT techniques. It can be used in the context of performance assessment to examine other important values that have ramifications both for scholarship and for actual practice. These exogenous criteria can be used to select exemplary districts and perform an analysis quite similar to that done when the criterion was endogenous. This chapter also demonstrated a SWLS using two criterion variables; by combining the two criterion variables into a single index, SWAT was generalized to any situation with multiple selection criteria.

6.9 References

Anyon, Jean. 1995. "Race, Social Class and Educational Reform in an Inner-City School." *Teachers College Record* 97: 69–94.

Burtless, Gary. 1996. *Does Money Matter? The Effect of School Resources on Student Achievement and Adult Success.* Washington, D.C.: Brookings Institution.

Downs, Anthony. 1967. *Inside Bureaucracy.* Boston: Little, Brown.

Frederickson, H. George. 1997. *The Spirit of Public Administration.* San Francisco: Jossey-Bass.

Garaway, G. B. 1995. "The Equity/Excellence Dialectic: Pluralism and the Impact of Educational Reform." *Equity & Excellence in Education,* 28: 65–72.

Goodsell, Charles T. 1989. "Balancing Competing Values." In *Handbook of Public Administration,* edited by James Perry. San Francisco: Jossey-Bass.

6 Equity Versus Excellence in Organizations 117

Hanushek, Eric A. 1996. "School Resources and Student Performance." In *Does Money Matter? The Effect of School Resources on Student Achievement and Adult Success,* edited by Gary Burtless. Washington, D.C.: Brookings Institution.

Hanushek, Eric A. 1989. "Expenditures, Efficiency, and Equity in Education: the Federal Government's Role." *American Economic Review* 79: 46–51.

Katz, Daniel, and Robert L. Kahn. 1966. *The Social Psychology of Organizations.* New York: Wiley.

Katz, Michael B. 1992. "Chicago School Reform as History." *Teachers College Record* 94: 56–72.

Lipsky, Michael. 1980. *Street-Level Bureaucracy: Dilemmas of the Individual in Public Services.* New York: Russell Sage Foundation.

Meier, Kenneth J., and Joseph Stewart, Jr. 1992. "Active Representation in Educational Bureaucracies: Policy Impacts." *American Review of Public Administration* 22: 157–171.

Meier, Kenneth J., and Joseph Stewart, Jr. 1991. *The Politics of Hispanic Education.* Albany, NY: SUNY Press.

Murphy, Joseph. 1989. "Is There Equity in Educational Reform?" *Educational Leadership* 46: 32–33.

Oakes, Jeannie. 1985. *Keeping Track: How Schools Structure Inequality.* New Haven, CT: Yale University Press.

Okun, Arthur. 1976. *Equality Versus Efficiency: The Big Tradeof.* Washington, D.C.: Brookings Institution.

Perrow, Charles. 1970. *Organizational Analysis: A Sociological View.* Belmont, CA: Brooks/Cole.

Polinard, J. L., Robert D. Wrinkle, Tomas Longoria, and Norman E. Binder. 1994. *Electoral Structure and Urban Policy: The Impact on Mexican American Communities.* Armonk, NY: M. E. Sharpe, Inc.

Polinard, J. L., Robert D. Wrinkle, and Kenneth J. Meier. 1995. "The Influence of Educational and Political Resources on Minority Students." *Journal of Negro Education* 64: 463–74.

Rainey, Hal G. 1997. *Understanding and Managing Public Organizations.* Second edition. San Francisco: Jossey-Bass.

Simon, Herbert A. 1957. *Administrative Behavior.* Second edition. New York: The Free Press.

Theilemann, Gregory S., and Joseph Stewart, Jr. 1996. "A Demand Side Perspective on the Importance of Representative Bureaucracy." *Public Administration Review* 56: 168–73.

Thompson, Frank J. 1976. "Minority Groups in Public Bureaucracies." *Administration and Society* 8: 201–226.

Thompson, James D. 1967. *Organizations in Action.* New York: McGraw-Hill.

Tyack, David B. 1974. *The One Best System: A History of American Urban Education.* Cambridge, MA: Harvard University Press.

Waldo, Dwight. 1971. *Public Administration in a Time of Turbulence.* San Francisco: Chandler Publishing Co.

Waller, George. 1997. "For the Want of a Modem and a Comfortable Chair: School Facilities and State Education Performance." Paper presented at the annual meeting of the Midwest Political Science Association, Chicago.

Chapter 7
SWAT in Pooled Analysis[1]

Kevin B. Smith, Kenneth J. Meier, Jeff Gill

7.1 Introduction

Numerous datasets in policy analysis and public administration are pooled datasets in which an individual organization might be represented more than once because several years of data are included. These can be panel or nonpanel configurations: individual cases explicitly tracked across time units or simply aggregations. The previous chapters have demonstrated the utility of substantively weighted analytical techniques (SWAT) in cross-sectional data; thus far there has been no work applying the technique to pooled datasets. Yet SWAT seems particularly suited to pooled analysis because of its ability to identify specific subgroups within a large, more complicated setting. In essence, the primary problem of pooled analysis (complicated error structures) is where SWAT gets its explanatory horsepower. Especially given the increasing popularity of pooled analysis (see Baltagi 1995), applying SWAT techniques in this area is likely to have a large payoff.

This chapter will do two things. First, it will lay down the basic logic of applying SWAT to pooled datasets and suggest a series of SWAT approaches that analysts of pooled data may find useful. Second, it will follow through on these suggestions

---

[1]This chapter was originally developed as Kevin B. Smith, "The Full, and Then Some, Prison Blues: A Substantively Weighted Least Squares Analysis of the Politics of Incarceration," at the 1998 annual meeting of the Midwest Political Science Association, April, Chicago, IL.

119

120   Kevin B. Smith, Kenneth J. Meier, Jeff Gill

with practical applications using an existing pooled dataset already analyzed by traditional pooling techniques.

In a change of pace, SWAT techniques will be used to analyze one of the most contentious and controversial policy questions faced by state policy makers—what can government do to control and reduce violent crime? Given the intense political (and academic) divisions over what causes crime and how it can be controlled, such an effort is almost certainly fated to be judged a failure by some. The bottom line is that SWAT will certainly benefit policy analysis that uses pooled datasets. Following the analysis of crime, we return to our education example for a second pooled illustration.

7.2 Zen and the Art of Pooling

Pooling generically refers to creating datasets that combine or "pool" observations on N cross-sectional units over t time periods (these are also called panel models; see Baltagi 1995, Sayrs 1989 for typical descriptions). For expository purposes, we assume a dataset where $N > T$.[2] In their general form, such models differ from a regular cross-sectional or time series model only in the appearance of a double subscript, that is:

$$Y_{it} = \alpha + X_{it}\beta + \mu_{it}. \tag{7.1}$$

The subscript denotes an observation on the ith cross-sectional unit at time t. Of particular concern to pooled analysis is the error process generated by such equations. These are generally assumed to take the following form:

$$\mu_{it} = u_i + v_{it} \tag{7.2}$$

where u_i is an unobservable unit-specific effect and v_{it} is the "usual" residual that varies randomly by cross section and across time. The obvious challenges posed by pooled analysis are the zero mean and constant variance requirements for the residuals in standard linear regression as assumed by the Gauss-Markov theorem. For a variety of reasons these assumptions are unlikely to hold, and the consequences for the reliability of the ordinary least squared (OLS) estimates can be severe (Stimson 1985; Sayrs 1989; Baltagi 1995; Dielman 1989). In practice, pooled analysis often is a matter of hammering out as much contamination from the error process as possible and "living" with what remains.

There are a variety of common approaches to obtaining this irreducible minimum, and various estimating strategies have been developed to achieve it (see

---

[2]Datasets where $T > N$, or what are often called narrow but deep pools, are amenable to time series techniques that are more sophisticated than the techniques presented here for shallow but wide pools. As a result, we leave the direct application of SWAT to long time series for future research.

Stimson 1985). The central concern of these efforts is efficiency—all estimation techniques generally produce unbiased and consistent parameter estimates (Pindyck and Rubinfeld 1991, p. 227). The search for efficiency, however, is not without a price. For example, a common approach to dealing with unit effects—contamination coming from $\mathbf{u}_i$—is to "fix" this error into a series of $N - 1$ dummy variables (what Stimson calls the least squares with dummy variables, or LSDV, model). Although this approach may solve one problem, it often introduces others. Common examples are a severe loss of degrees of freedom, and multicollinearity as the dummies become hopelessly entangled with the regressors of interest.

In a recent development in the search for better ways to estimate parameters from pooled datasets, Beck and Katz (1995) argue that the cures applied to pooled models are often worse than the original disease. Their basic prescription is to stick with OLS, lag the outcome variable as a way to bring the dynamic element of the data to the fore (and consequently control serial correlation), and "panel correct" the standard errors.[3] There is something to be said for this approach, and it may end up as a standard operating procedure for pooled analysis. But even here, there may be problems. A lagged outcome variable bears some relationship to the error process by design (Baltagi 1995, p. 125). It is also likely to focus on short-term effects at the expense of ignoring long-term effects, thus avoiding a primary advantage of an $N > T$ dataset (dynamic models are in essence models of differences, and cross-sectional dominance is better suited to examining long-range relationships; see Pindyck and Rubinfeld 1991, Baltagi and Griffin 1984). In addition, such lags are often "variance hogs," and may mask real relationships the other regressors have with the outcome variable. The bottom line is that there is no one best pooled estimator, but a variety of choices available to address a number of problems (see Stimson 1985).

All the approaches to generating estimators from pooled datasets are essentially efforts to get the error process to "behave." SWAT requires an approach to errors that is fundamentally at odds with conventional wisdom; Chapter 1 refers to this shift from traditional regression philosophy as the "Zen" of policy analysis. The Zen of pooling begins with a radical break from the primary goal of getting the error process to look normal. SWAT does not seek to make errors behave—it is premised on the notion that the "misbehavior" should be explored rather than eliminated. Systematic patterns in $\mathbf{u}_i$ or $\mathbf{v}_{it}$ are not something to be "hammered out" or assumed away, but something to deliberately chase. The logic is that the residuals tell us something about a unit, time period, or observation that is different; and this difference might tell us something we would otherwise miss.

---

[3]Beck and Katz (1995) are careful to limit their work to datasets where $T > N$, recognizing that the problems in $N > T$ datasets are often different (e.g., serial correlation is less of a problem in "short and fat" datasets). However, the two are formal equivalents and the Beck and Katz technique has been freely adapted to $N > T$ datasets (e.g., Fording 1997). Given its popularity as an estimation technique regardless of dataset structure, we include it here even though we focus on the $N > T$ case.

This, of course, is not exactly a revelatory insight. For example, as Stimson's (1985) treatment of LSDV makes clear, dummy variables representing unit effects have long been recognized as having something substantive to say. But while analysts faced with an array of significant unit-specific dummies can isolate and estimate a unit effect, they have little guidance on exactly why the particular cross section is different. SWAT is designed to provide this guidance.

The starting point for SWAT is that policy analysts are not always interested in the average case—the central concern of traditional regression techniques—but rather in above average cases. What do the above average states do differently from everyone else, and what separates the outliers from the average case? The application of SWAT to pooled models has implications both for substantive policy analysis and for the methodology of pooling—the former because pools offer a richer data environment to exploit the advantages of SWAT, the latter because the primary disadvantage of pools (error structures that "misbehave") are just what the SWAT analyst is deliberately looking for rather than deliberately seeking to avoid.

The leap from the cross-sectional to the pooled case involves some modifications of the original SWAT process. Generally, the analyst with pooled data is hoping to achieve an error structure where all the disturbances are homoscedastic and with the same variance across time and individuals. In the generic $N > T$ case, unit effects are a prime focus, as autocorrelation is a less likely source of contamination (see Stimson 1985). In this case, there appear to be two basic approaches to adopting SWAT to a pooled dataset, each accounting for one of the two expected sources of variation in the error process.

Basically, instead of a single weighting scheme, a pooled model calls for two: one based on $\mathbf{u}_i$, and one on $\mathbf{v}_{it}$. The former would, in essence, be used to examine why some cross sections differ from others; the latter, to examine why individual observations differ from others. Rather than trying to eliminate these errors as nuisances, the idea is to pursue both in an effort to see why they are there to begin with.[4] Regardless, all the potential advantages associated with SWAT would apply to such an approach, but to an even higher degree—the information in the unusual cases likely to be highlighted in a pooled error process would be taken advantage of rather than suppressed. The remainder of this chapter will present two cases, one involving crime and one using education data, to explore and highlight these advantages.

---

[4]There is also a case for a third weighting scheme, i.e., one based on time periods. This situation is likely to be more of a concern in $T > N$ datasets. In the case presented here, we averaged Studentized residuals by year and none of these means was greater in absolute value than 0.7. In other words, whatever separated high- from low-performing cases had little to do with particular time periods. Although we thus ignore this potential weighting scheme, we strongly recommend that analysts applying SWAT techniques to pooled data get similar empirical verification before adopting this strategy, and not simply assume away potential effects from time.

7.3 The Full—and Then Some—Prison Blues

During the past two decades, crime and punishment have become increasingly central concerns of state policy makers. Beginning in the mid-1970s, the dominant thinking about criminal justice policy switched from rehabilitation to deterrence. By the mid-1980s, crime policy became overtly politicized, with policy makers increasingly separating themselves from research to engage in ideological duels over who was the "toughest on crime." The upshot of these developments has been a massive increase in prison populations, with incarceration rates rising from 110 per 100,000 population in the mid-1970s to 427 per 100,000 in 1996 (see Blumstein 1998, 1997).

The wisdom of these developments has been intensely debated by scholars across several disciplines, and the stakes involved are considerable. Two decades ago, corrections accounted for between 1 and 2 percent of state budgets. Currently it accounts for between 8 and 10 percent and is the fastest growing category of state expenditure (Greenwood 1998). Incarcerations have grown during a time when crime rates have fluctuated around fairly stable means, or even undergone slight decreases. The debate revolves around a central unresolved question: Are the benefits of incarcerating ever-increasing proportions of the population outweighed by the concurrent financial and social costs?

Although the costs—at least in budgetary terms—can be easily reckoned, the benefits are controversial. The central objective of criminal justice policy is to reduce crime and keep law-abiding citizens safe. Is this benefit achieved by increasing incarceration rates? The theoretical work in this area essentially reduces the options for achieving this policy goal to two. As Devine et al. (1988, p. 408) put it, "governments counter crime with a carrot-and-stick approach." The carrot takes the form of placative attempts at social control such as higher welfare expenditures. The stick consists of threats and punishments such as longer prison sentences. "Stick"-based policies are largely based on deterrence theory, which views criminals as rational actors who will choose not to engage in deviant behavior if the costs for doing so can be made to outweigh the benefits (e.g., Ehrlich 1975). "Carrot"-based policies are founded on the competing paradigm of determinism, exemplified in the criminological literature by strain theory, which views sociocultural, biological, environmental, and developmental factors as primary determinants of criminal behavior (for surveys see Chaires and Stitt 1994, Agnew 1995).

There is a vast multidisciplinary literature examining the differing policy prescriptions that spring from these approaches to the causes of crime, but it has produced little consensus (see Skolnick 1995, Walker 1985). The lines dividing scholars on this question are sharp. Petersilia (1995) argues, "tough-on-crime legislation has political appeal, (but) it finds almost no support among criminal justice practitioners and scholars." DiIulio (1995, p. 15) replies to such arguments by saying, "Apparently, it takes a Ph.D. in Criminology to doubt that keeping dangerous criminals incarcerated cuts crime." As locking up criminals is rarely politically unpopular, it is the latter sentiment that has been translated into policy.

But does locking up criminals cut crime rates? The less than satisfactory answer is that we are not really sure. We do know, however, that crime rates vary considerably from community to community, and from state to state. A logical first step in moving towards policy prescription is to be able to explain the variation in crime rates. If we can isolate variables manipulable by policy makers that have both theoretical and empirical causal links with crime, we are a step closer to prescriptive policy conclusions. A large literature has devoted itself to explaining variation in crime rates. Unfortunately, it too has produced little consensus, and the record is littered with wildly varying model specifications reporting differing or even contradictory impacts of this or that variable. Land et al. (1990) and McCall et al. (1992) undertook an exhaustive examination of this literature and parsed out a generalized set of structural covariates of crime rates. The resulting model has three important characteristics. First, it was theoretically supportable. Second, with minor exceptions, it produced results that were invariant to unit of analysis. Third, with minor exceptions, it produced results that were invariant to the time period studied.

Recently Smith (1997) adopted the Land model as a platform for assessing crime policy impacts in a pooled state-level dataset. The objective was to model homicide rates between 1975 and 1990 using the Land model, and add variables representing the deterrence and determinism arguments to assess their effectiveness. The findings were mixed. Social welfare policies (Smith used commitment to income equalization and commitment to primary and secondary education) seemed to have some long-term negative relationships with homicide rates. From this Smith inferred that policies based in determinism were effective long-term crime control strategies. Prison population was a positive predictor of homicide rates, and his main inference here was that recent deterrence-based work arguing that the causal relationship running from prisons to crime was one-way (at least in the short term) was almost certainly wrong. But Smith also picked up persistent negative relationships for variables measuring the presence of a death penalty and the number of executions (although these were not 95% CI bounded away from zero), which did fit with the deterrence argument. In short, Smith (1997) managed to arrive at half of an answer to the central policy question: Does locking up more people lead to less crime? No, but the deterrence arguments that underpin this approach may have validity in other areas.

These models did provide strong empirical evidence for determinism-based policies (a rarity in the extant literature). But the contribution hardly represents definitive empirical closure to the prescriptive policy questions surrounding crime policy. However, methodologically speaking, there seemed to be few other avenues to pursue with the dataset at hand. Smith (1997) used not one estimation technique, but three, and they all yielded similar results. Searching for the average impact in the average state in the average year, Smith came up with an answer that essentially averaged the findings of the existing literature. SWAT's promise is to offer a little more prescriptive illumination to such problems.

7.4 Looking at the Data

We use state-level data pooled from 1975 to 1990. The outcome variable is homicide rate measured by homicides per 100,000 of the state population. We posit eleven explanatory variables in the specification. The measurement and data source for each of these variables are outlined in the chapter addendum. Two key explanatory variables are investigated in detail: population structure (an index from density and size) and resource deprivation (an index from percent black, percent in poverty, and per capita income).

The relationship between homicide rates, population structure, and resource deprivation is shown in quite a dramatic fashion in the *casement display*[5] provided in Figure 7.1. This graphical exploratory data analysis tool gives a scatterplot of murder rates against the population structure variable for six increasing (equal sized) levels of resource deprivation. The ranges of these six levels are indicated by the widthof the gray bands along the top of the figure. The figure is constructed so the lower left-hand panel corresponds to the lowest level of resource deprivation, $[-2 : -1]$, and the categories increase moving to the right on the lower row and then up to the upper left-hand corner and across the upper row. Thus the panel that corresponds to the highest level of resource deprivation, $[1:4]$, is the upper right-hand panel. Therefore associate the wide gray band in the upper right-hand corner of top (wide) window, indicating a range of resource deprivation, with the upper rightmost box containing a scatterplot with points concentrated in the middle of the graph. Often additional trend indicators such as regression lines and smoothers are added within the casements, but in this case the effect is so pronounced that no such device is necessary.

It is evident in the first two panels that there is no noticeable relationship between murder and population structure at lower levels of resource deprivation, that is, wealthier cases. However, as resource deprivation gradually increases, a distinctly linear relationship between population structure and murder clearly develops. Finally, at the highest level of resource deprivation, the relationship between population structure and murder is a tight ball structure, which implies that there is small covariance in this relationship for high levels of resource deprivation. These cases are clustered around zero of the population structure variable,

---

[5]A closely related tool is the *conditioning plot*, a casement display in which the categories are overlapped by some arbitrary amount. Overlapping is often used for small sample sizes.

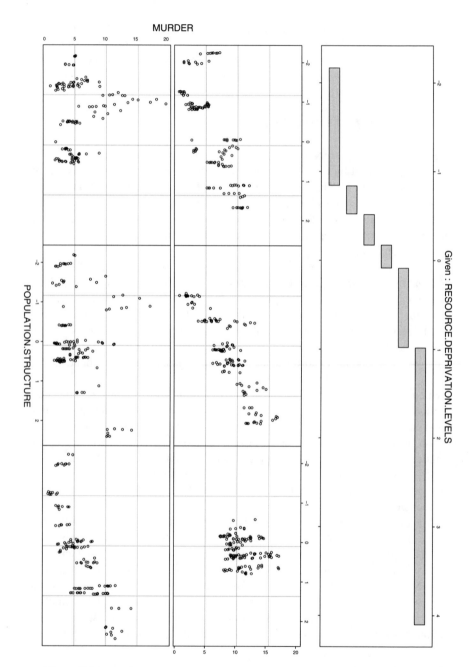

Figure 7.1 Casement Display, Homicides vs Population Structure by Resource Deprivation

but have the highest average murder rate of any level of resource deprivation. This finding is very interesting because it provides evidence that the relationship between population structure and murder is profoundly affected by varying levels of resource deprivation.

7.5 Applying SWAT to the Data

Linear model results are outlined in Table 7.1. For a defense of the linear specification and measures used see Smith 1997, Land et al. 1990, McCall et al. 1992.

The results indicate that the primary contributors to homicide rates are population structure (from population density and population size), resource deprivation (from percent of black population, percent below poverty line, and per capita income), and prison population. The latter is the only variable directly manipulable by policy makers—and it is in the "wrong" direction, indicating that larger prison populations are associated with higher homicide rates. Although not wielding the impact of these three, other variables representing criminal justice policies do show some evidence of curbing violent crime.

Lagged education commitment and resource equalization both have negative coefficients, indicating that long-term commitment to the social welfare of young people pays off in a less violent society (the income equalization variable has a

Table 7.1   Determinants of Homicide Rates: Linear Model

Explanatory Variable	Outcome Variable = Exam Pass Rates		
	Coefficient	Std. Error	95% CI
Intercept	0.89029	1.54008	[−2.12826: 3.90885]
Population Structure	1.38173	0.09208	[1.20125: 1.56221]
Resource Deprivation	1.08865	0.14523	[0.80400: 1.37330]
Divorce Rate	0.65064	0.04754	[0.55746: 0.74382]
Age	0.08313	0.03680	[0.01101: 0.15526]
Unemployment	0.04177	0.04075	[−0.03810: 0.12164]
South	1.07350	0.31377	[0.45852: 1.68848]
Death Penalty	0.16379	0.21084	[−0.24945: 0.57703]
Prison Population	0.00805	0.00147	[0.00517: 0.01092]
Income Equalization	−0.04510	0.02982	[−0.10354: 0.01334]
Education Commitment	−0.34708	0.09869	[−0.54050:−0.15366]
Number of Executions	−0.17887	0.11054	[−0.39552: 0.03779]

Multiple $R^2 = 0.6374$
$F = 125.9$ on 11 and 788 degrees of freedom
Residual Standard Error = 2.322 on 788 degrees of freedom

128   *Kevin B. Smith, Kenneth J. Meier, Jeff Gill*

95% confidence interval that just barely covers zero). The death penalty coefficient is unreliable, possibly because the presence of a death penalty has little or no deterrent effect (although we can make no such claim given this model and these data). On the other hand, the number of executions in a given year does seem to have a slight deterrent impact. The results, in other words, are mixed—providing some evidence for deterrence and deterministic policies but mostly counseling caution in prescriptive policy terms.[6]

SWAT is not an appropriate technique for all situations; two rules to govern its use (see Chapter 1). The first of these is normative: SWAT is appropriate when an analyst is interested in high (or low) performers. SWAT is essentially designed to incorporate these values into the analysis. The present case would seem to fit the normative rule—many policy makers and citizens in general are interested in programs that keep crime rates low. The second rule is empirical—is the residual variation of a model meaningful? This question is assessed by examining the standard error of the regression to see whether it is substantively meaningful in terms of policy. The standard error of the regression reported in the standard linear model is 2.3. Is this meaningful in policy terms? Between 1975 and 1990, the mean state homicide rate was 7.17, and the mean state population was approximately 4.6 million, which translates to 330 homicides per year. Dropping the homicide rate by 2.3 reduces that number to 224, and increasing the rate by 2.3 increases the number of homicides to 435—a spread of more than 200 lives lost (or not) in violent criminal acts. In substantive policy terms, the variation seems meaningful.

This point is underlined by Figure 7.2. The first panel shows a plot of actual homicide rates against the rates predicted by the model reported in Table 7.1. The plot shows a reasonably good fit with the data, but there remains a good deal of upside scatter about the regression line. There is a prima facie case that this scatter may contain useful information that the model in Table 7.1 is not reporting. Some states (e.g., Maryland, Michigan, New York) are consistently above the regression line, indicating they have higher homicide rates than expected given the inputs of the model. Other states (e.g., Iowa, Minnesota, Ohio) are consistently below the regression line, indicating they have lower homicide rates than expected. What are states with higher than expected homicide rates doing "wrong"? What are states with lower than expected homicide rates doing "right"? The answers to these questions may provide guidelines to prescriptive policy. In addition, the normal-quantile plot (Panel 3) shows a worrisome amount of upward curvature. This shape indicates that the data are somewhat right-skewed, supporting the conclusions from Panel 1, as well as the residual dependence plot in Panel 2 (note the high side outliers and the scale).

---

[6]These results are slightly different from those reported in Smith 1997. Smith's model included time dummies, which are not included here. Dropping the time dummies has some impact on the magnitude of the coefficients, although the models lead to the same general inferences.

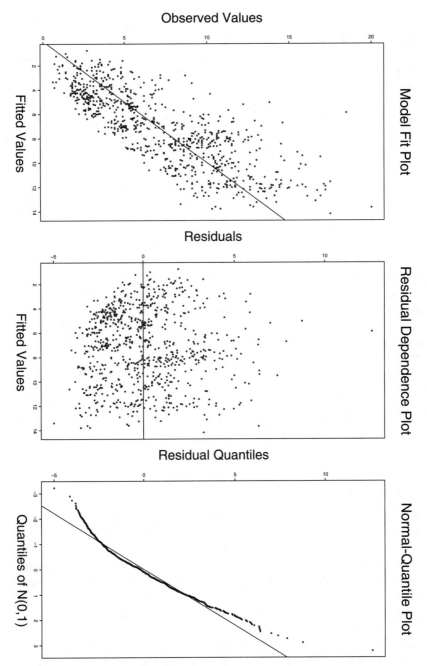

Figure 7.2 Diagnostics: Linear Model

130   *Kevin B. Smith, Kenneth J. Meier, Jeff Gill*

In the pooled case, there are some complications to the standard SWAT procedure as outlined in previous chapters. The first is the decision on how to calculate the weights. If we are interested in the units—in this case, the states—it makes sense to average the residuals by unit. So the weighting scheme would be based on state means; that is, if a state had a mean Studentized residual of 0.7 or higher, it is designated as a high-performing case. This method essentially is an attempt to use the $\mathbf{u}_i$ as the source of variation in the residuals. But a case can also be made for ignoring the units and simply calculating the weights on the basis of the untouched Studentized residuals, which allows states to be designated high performers in one year and low in another. In substantive policy terms, this might make sense. For example, if there is a deterrent effect associated with the number of executions in a state, and the number fluctuates from year to year, the latter weighting scheme may be better equipped to assess its impact. This is an attempt to use $\mathbf{v}_i$ as the source of variation. This chapter will present both approaches and then comment on when one might be more appropriate than the other in the conclusion.

The second issue has to do with designating the "high performers." Of interest in this case, of course, are the low performers—states with lower homicide rates than the average case. At the same time, the states with higher than predicted crime rates are also interesting since they are likely to reveal more clearly how not to fight crime. Figure 7.2, in fact, shows the biggest outliers tend to be states with higher than expected homicide rates. Both approaches will be presented in this chapter.

Accordingly, Studentized residuals were saved from the model reported in Table 7.1 and used as the basis for four SWLS analyses: two using the "usual" Studentized residuals (one using $+0.7$ as the basis of the weighting scheme, one using -0.7), and two using the cross-sectional means of Studentized residuals (again one based on $+0.7$ and one on -0.7).

7.5.1 A Note of Caution

In using SWAT techniques, we have consistently argued that we are looking for differences in relationships rather than differences based on the X variables. Such an approach fits cross-sectional regression well but is less likely to fit a pooled relationship simply because in a pooled relationship the errors are unlikely to be unrelated to each other. As an illustration, the errors for a single organization/state are likely to be correlated with each other simply because the organization operates with the same set of personnel, the same set of rules, etc., year after year.

In doing previous SWAT analyses, we started by comparing the sets of organizations on the X variables. A similar comparison is done in Table 7.2 and demonstrates that indeed the two sets of agencies differ from each other in terms of X variables. Table 7.2, containing the low crime states, shows that those states

7 SWAT in Pooled Analysis   131

Table 7.2   Comparison of Low Crime States to All Others

Explanatory Variable	All	Raw Weights			Mean Weights		
		Mean	Std. Error	t-statistic	Mean	Std. Error	t-statistic
Murder Rate	7.1722	4.9613	0.1749	9.9943	4.6006	0.1747	11.6313
Population Structure	−0.0040	−0.0128	0.0429	0.1569	0.0980	0.0484	−1.7016
Resource Deprivation	0.0000	0.0428	0.0573	−0.6351	−0.2017	0.0542	3.1162
Divorce Rate	5.3049	5.5865	0.1223	−2.0014	5.5534	0.1013	−2.0227
Age	41.2832	41.7006	0.1582	−2.1537	40.7410	0.1973	2.3908
Unemployment	6.8146	7.1965	0.1619	−2.1182	7.0501	0.1580	−1.3322
Death Penalty	0.7100	0.6577	0.0320	1.4622	0.6000	0.0390	2.6095
Prison Population	155.1462	163.7387	5.9630	−1.2891	121.3625	4.3208	6.4374
Income Equalization	15.1127	14.6514	0.2730	1.4676	16.6336	0.3183	−4.2928
Education Commitment	5.1550	5.2955	0.0494	−2.2990	5.3662	0.0686	−2.7285
Number of Executions	0.1788	0.1126	0.0287	1.6210	0.0438	0.0185	3.9205

that consistently have lower crime levels (the mean residual measure) than predicted are different from all other states as well as those states that have lower rates at least one year (the raw residual measure). With 800 cases, however, even small differences are 95% CI bounded away from zero. For example, the age difference for raw residuals (41.3 versus 41.7) is rather trivial. These relatively modest differences, even though 95% CI bounded away from zero, are unlikely to make dramatic differences in the model. Table 7.2 also provides t-statistics for the mean difference between the raw weight means and the overall mean and between the mean weight mean and the overall mean.

7.5.2 The Winners: The Low Crime States

In comparing SWAT results, we will focus on the five key policy variables—capital punishment, the number of executions, prison population, income equalization, and educational commitment. Tables 7.3 and 7.4 present the final weighted results for the low crime states. For both sets of states, the prison population variable remains positive and 95% CI bounded away from zero, and the death penalty variable also becomes positive and 95% CI bounded away from zero. In both cases the coefficient for the number of executions is effectively zero. In combination, these findings suggest that low crime states are not achieving their status via deterrence-based policies. All such policies are either 95% covering zero as predictors or 95% CI bounded away from zero in the wrong direction.

On the carrot side, both sets of results have income equalization coefficients that remain essentially the same as the OLS coefficients. The one key policy difference is in educational investment. The consistently low crime states (Table 7.4) are able to obtain approximately 82% more impact from their commitment to education (their slightly higher educational expenditures also add to this difference). The

132 Kevin B. Smith, Kenneth J. Meier, Jeff Gill

Table 7.3 Determinants of Homicide Rates:
SWLS Estimates—Low Crime, Raw Weights

Explanatory Variable	Outcome Variable = Murder Rates		
	Coefficient	Std. Error	95% CI
Intercept	2.10063	1.40019	[−0.64374: 4.84499]
Population Structure	1.35297	0.09376	[1.16919: 1.53674]
Resource Deprivation	0.91708	0.13901	[0.64463: 1.18953]
Divorce Rate	0.56750	0.04329	[0.48264: 0.65235]
Age	0.03980	0.03502	[−0.02883: 0.10843]
Unemployment	−0.01640	0.02964	[−0.07450: 0.04169]
South	1.35455	0.25442	[0.85588: 1.85322]
Death Penalty	0.29644	0.16059	[−0.01832: 0.61120]
Prison Population	0.00624	0.00119	[0.00391: 0.00858]
Income Equalization	−0.04481	0.02362	[−0.09111: 0.00149]
Education Commitment	−0.39184	0.08622	[−0.56083:−0.22286]
Number of Executions	0.05118	0.11609	[−0.17636: 0.27872]

Multiple $R^2 = 0.7055$
$F = 171.6$ on 11 and 788 degrees of freedom
Residual Standard Error = 1.022 on 788 degrees of freedom

Table 7.4 Determinants of Homicide Rates:
SWLS Estimates—Low Crime, Mean Weights

Explanatory Variable	Outcome Variable = Murder Rates		
	Coefficient	Std. Error	95% CI
Intercept	1.57856	1.48182	[−1.32581: 4.48293]
Population Structure	1.22271	0.09394	[1.03859: 1.40684]
Resource Deprivation	0.96455	0.16393	[0.64326: 1.28585]
Divorce Rate	0.56276	0.05094	[0.46291: 0.66261]
Age	0.09086	0.03827	[0.01584: 0.16587]
Unemployment	−0.05010	0.03471	[−0.11814: 0.01794]
South	1.57271	0.32776	[0.93029: 2.21512]
Death Penalty	0.29548	0.16414	[−0.02624: 0.61720]
Prison Population	0.00844	0.00143	[0.00564: 0.01124]
Income Equalization	−0.04435	0.02267	[−0.08879: 0.00009]
Education Commitment	−0.62299	0.08788	[−0.79524:−0.45075]
Number of Executions	0.04487	0.13234	[−0.21451: 0.30425]

Multiple $R^2 = 0.6597$
$F = 138.9$ on 11 and 788 degrees of freedom
Residual Standard Error = 0.9760951 on 788 degrees of freedom

states with occasionally low crime rates (Table 7.3) get only slightly more from educational expenditures (+13%).

The control variables also merit some comment. The low crime states generally have smaller slopes, suggesting that these states overcome a negative environment better than average states do. Such results might occur because of other policy variables not included in the model. The consistently low crime states (mean residuals, Table 7.4) do not get as great a reduction in the slopes as the occasional low crime states, but their impacts are generally a bit less.

These general findings are confirmed by the slope change graphs for these regressions (Figure 7.3). Both figures show the executions variable dropping to zero. The death penalty lines are somewhat misleading since the slope is in the wrong direction. The only strong finding is that investments in education matter for those states that have consistently low crime rates.

This set of results suggests that the mean weights are probably going to be more useful to the policy analyst than the raw weights. Using the mean requires that the state/organization be able to consistently outperform the regression model. Although it may be relatively easy to get good results once, doing so consistently year after year gives one more faith that the organizations really are better organizations and not organizations that have gotten a break from their environment (see Chapter 5).

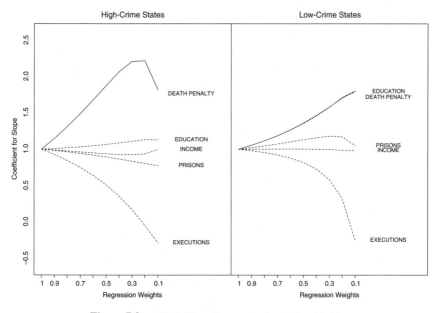

Figure 7.3   SWLS, Slope Changes for Low Crime Model

7.5.3 The Losers: High Crime States

Table 7.5 compares the high crime states to all other states on the values of the X variables and provides t-statistics for the mean difference. Here a major difference appears between the raw scored and the mean scored states. When the raw weights are used, there are no 95% CI bounded away from zero differences between the high crime states and all other states (although unemployment is marginally 95% CI bounded away from zero). The states that consistently have higher crime rates, however, are 95% CI bounded away from zero different from all other states on seven of the ten explanatory variables. The net effect of these differences, however, is not consistent. The high crime states have less dense population structures, lower divorce rates, older populations, higher prison populations, more equal incomes, and spend more on education (relationships consistent with less crime); these states also have higher unemployment rates and are less likely to have a death penalty.

Tables 7.6 and 7.7 show the SWLS results for the high crime states. The striking finding of these tables is that the policy process in high crimes states clearly works in a different manner than it does in the low crime states. The carrot policies now all have 95% confidence intervals covering zero. In these states there is no evidence from these data and this model that income equalization or greater long-term expenditures on education matter. None of the four coefficients is statistically distinct from zero.

In the deterrence policies, additional differences show up. Prison population remains 95% CI bounded away from zero and positive, implying that in all types of states increasing the incarceration rate cannot deter crime. In the high crime states, the slope sign on the death penalty reverses and becomes negative although not 95% CI bounded away from zero. The key deterrent impact is the number of executions. This variable grows in importance in high crime states; the SWLS

Table 7.5   Comparison of High Crime States to All Others

Explanatory Variable	All	Raw Weights			Mean Weights		
		Mean	Std. Error	t-statistic	Mean	Std. Error	t-statistic
Murder Rate	7.1722	4.9803	0.1751	9.8995	9.5594	0.3195	−6.8782
Population Structure	−0.0040	−0.0189	0.0432	0.2666	−0.2174	0.1046	1.9319
Resource Deprivation	0.0000	0.0378	0.0572	−0.5612	−0.0823	0.0934	0.8241
Divorce Rate	5.3049	5.5964	0.1222	−2.0738	4.8414	0.1510	2.7887
Age	41.2832	41.7123	0.1580	−2.2167	42.6960	0.3058	−4.3382
Unemployment	6.8146	7.1902	0.1612	−2.0898	7.6672	0.2168	−3.6920
Death Penalty	0.7100	0.6592	0.0319	1.4231	0.4766	0.0445	4.9348
Prison Population	155.1462	163.6099	5.9375	−1.2741	177.5938	8.1188	−2.5957
Income Equalization	15.1127	14.6563	0.2718	1.4568	15.5126	0.2825	−1.2398
Education Commitment	5.1550	5.3054	0.0502	−2.4361	5.5344	0.1254	−2.9070
Number of Executions	0.1788	0.1121	0.0286	1.6369	0.1484	0.0780	0.3642

7 SWAT in Pooled Analysis   135

Table 7.6   Determinants of Homicide Rates:
SWLS Estimates—High Crime, Raw Weights

| Explanatory Variable | Outcome Variable = Murder Rates | | |
	Coefficient	Std. Error	95% CI
Intercept	−1.17797	1.63159	[−4.37588: 2.01995]
Population Structure	1.44879	0.08365	[1.28484: 1.61274]
Resource Deprivation	1.14757	0.14734	[0.85879: 1.43636]
Divorce Rate	0.79881	0.04082	[0.71881: 0.87881]
Age	0.14690	0.03839	[0.07165: 0.22215]
Unemployment	0.09216	0.04503	[0.00390: 0.18043]
South	1.40208	0.35007	[0.71596: 2.08821]
Death Penalty	−0.18575	0.22764	[−0.63192: 0.26042]
Prison Population	0.00718	0.00147	[0.00429: 0.01007]
Income Equalization	−0.05587	0.03192	[−0.11843: 0.00669]
Education Commitment	−0.15207	0.09089	[−0.33022: 0.02607]
Number of Executions	−0.38986	0.10736	[−0.60029:−0.17943]

Multiple $R^2 = 0.6592$
$F = 138.5$ on 11 and 788 degrees of freedom
Residual Standard Error = 1.304 on 788 degrees of freedom

Table 7.7   Determinants of Homicide Rates:
SWLS Estimates—High Crime, Mean Weights

| Explanatory Variable | Outcome Variable = Murder Rates | | |
	Coefficient	Std. Error	95% CI
Intercept	−5.90941	1.92472	[−9.68186:−2.13696]
Population Structure	1.36823	0.09615	[1.17977: 1.55670]
Resource Deprivation	1.47932	0.17609	[1.13417: 1.82446]
Divorce Rate	0.58793	0.05542	[0.47930: 0.69656]
Age	0.24903	0.04419	[0.16242: 0.33564]
Unemployment	0.14774	0.04204	[0.06535: 0.23014]
South	0.92351	0.39417	[0.15094: 1.69608]
Death Penalty	−0.35861	0.23211	[−0.81356: 0.09633]
Prison Population	0.00765	0.00151	[0.00468: 0.01062]
Income Equalization	0.00050	0.03656	[−0.07116: 0.07216]
Education Commitment	−0.17930	0.09461	[−0.36474: 0.00615]
Number of Executions	−0.44820	0.11646	[−0.67647:−0.21993]

Multiple $R^2 = 0.587$
$F = 101.8$ on 11 and 788 degrees of freedom
Residual Standard Error = 1.238 on 788 degrees of freedom

136   Kevin B. Smith, Kenneth J. Meier, Jeff Gill

slope for the mean weight regression is 2.5 times the size of the OLS slope (for the raw weights it is 2.18 times the OLS slope). In states with consistently high murder rates, frequent executions appear to be associated with declines in the murder rate.

Before concluding that we have identified a set of states that conform only to the deterrence model, we should also mention the coefficient for unemployment. For the mean weights regression (Table 7.7), the slope for unemployment is a dramatic 3.5 times the size of the OLS slope. This finding suggests that employment policies (also a carrot) might have greater impact in high crime states; this is just a supposition, however, since the OLS slope does not reach 95% CI bounded away from zero status.

Overall, the sets of tables paint different pictures of low and high crime states. In high crime states, carrot policies other than employment show no evidence of an impact on murder rates but deterrence policies (executions) do. In low crime states, carrot policies have a positive impact, and deterrence policies show little or no evidence of an impact. These findings suggest a contingency approach to crime policy; what policies work effectively depend on the extent of the problem in the state. This makes intuitive sense; a household fire extinguisher is very effective on small household fires but would be virtually useless in a forest fire.

Heterogeneity in the policy situation (or the organizations' environment) structures the types of policies that can be effective.[7] Standard linear regression, by ignoring this heterogeneity, would not have revealed the different paths these sets of states were on. The most cogent illustration of the differences between the sets of states is Figure 7.3, showing the slope change graphs for two sets of states for the number of executions. In high crime states, the impact of executions rises to almost double and is 95% CI bounded away from zero; executions appear to have a deterrent effect. In low crime states, however, executions have less and less impact, eventually changing signs and being positively related to murder rates. In short, in low crime states, there is no evidence from these data and this model that executions have a deterrent effect.

The distinctive patterns for these two variables are confirmed in the slope change graph (Figure 7.3). All other slope change graphs are clustered together in the center of the graphs. The large and consistent changes in these two variables suggest a great deal of heterogeneity in their application in individual districts.

We have repeatedly advised practitioners of SWAT to look at various graphical and nongraphical diagnostics to check the validity of underlying assumptions. Figure 7.4 shows the now familiar graphical diagnostic suite for the four SWLS models developed in this section. It can immediately be seen that the models for

---

[7]For a policy theory based on the idea of heterogeneity, see Meier (1998). That paper presents a formal theory demonstrating why heterogeneity of preferences influences the effectiveness of policy instruments.

7 SWAT in Pooled Analysis 137

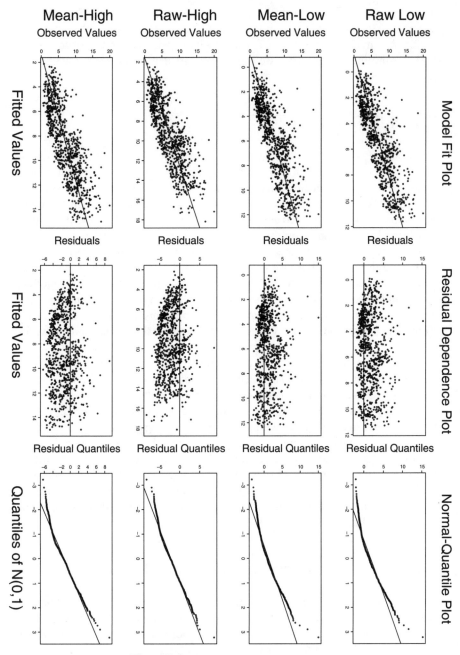

Figure 7.4 Diagnostics: Homicide Models

high performers are based on more reliable regression assumptions. The curvature apparent in the standard linear model (Figure 7.2) is still quite visible in the low-performing models. However, it appears to be considerably diminished for the high-performing models. Thus we should have greater confidence in the findings reported in Tables 7.6 and 7.7.

7.6 Path Dependence

Our example of crime policy suggests an interesting possible substantive use of SWAT. Low crime and high crime states appear to be affected by different sets of factors. This type of situation can occur in a policy realm when decisions early in a program life cut off options later in time. As an illustration, when the United States government initially regulated television, it decided to mix UHF and VHF stations. VHF (the lower numbers on the dial) were considered more desirable because reception was better, and many televisions were manufactured that received only channels 2 through 13. Because stations had to be located a certain distance apart to avoid signals bleeding into each other, this decision meant that a metropolitan area could have no more than 3 VHF stations. By limiting major metropolitan areas to no more than three of the "good" stations, this decision by the Federal Communications Commission guaranteed that no more than three major networks would exist; FCC decisions to increase competition were simply foreclosed by their earlier decision. Such was the case until satellite and cable technology improved to overcome this limitation. The phenomenon of early decisions limiting future decisions is called path dependence. Although path dependence could be examined in a variety of ways, SWAT might be useful. Some states might decide to fight crime with carrots and others with sticks. Either strategy requires an investment in bureaucracy and might limit the ability to change policies in the future. In cases such as this, one would expect that the relationships among the variables would be vastly different for one type of state versus the other. Because SWAT is sensitive to variations in slopes and it clusters groups of cases by how the data are arrayed rather than some existing criterion, it could be one way to verify that organizations are pursuing different paths in addressing a public policy.

7.7 A Second Example: Educational Performance

For a second example, we return to our running illustration of educational performance. Our dataset includes all schools in Texas with more than 1000 students for the years 1991 through 1996. A total of 376 schools meet this standard for all six years. The production function used is similar to that used in all other chapters. The outcome variable is the percentage of students who pass the standardized

TAAS exam. Explanatory variables include measures of poverty (percent black, Latino, and low-income students), measures of school resources (instructional funds, teacher salaries, state aid), and some school and teacher measures (gifted classes, class size, teacher experience, and percent of teachers with temporary certifications). In addition to these variables, each model will include a set of dummy variables to control for serial correlation. The dummy variables are crucial in this model because average scores rise and fall together as the test changes in individual years.

Before beginning the analysis, we should note that this set of schools is much different from the set used for other analyses in previous chapters. These are larger schools, more likely to be in major urban areas, and thus more difficult to change. As larger schools, they are also more likely to have diverse curricula and a larger range of course options. In addition, the school environment in Texas changed significantly between 1991 and 1996 with substantially increased immigration. The proportion of Latino students increased by about 10 percent in this time period with a similar increase, although not as large, in low-income students. The findings of this analysis, therefore, will differ in some respects from those in previous chapters.

Table 7.8 presents the OLS regression (including the serial correlation controls) for the production function. In general, all relationships are as expected. Negative relationships are found for percent black, percent Latino, and percent low-income students. Positive relationships exist for all funding variables—instructional funds, teacher salaries, and state aid. Teacher experience and gifted classes are positively related to performance, and class size and teacher noncertification are negatively related. All relationships are statistically significant (i.e., 95% CI bounded away from zero), but with 2256 cases, this is not a high standard.

To vary the analysis a bit, we now focus on high-performing schools and define that standard as scoring above a Studentized residual of 1.0 on average for all six years. This criterion eliminates schools that occasionally score well above expectations to focus on those that consistently score high relative to their inputs. A total of 36 schools meet this standard.

Table 7.9 compares the high-performing schools to the rest of the schools on all variables. Although with 2256 cases and a pooled structure that would enhance the likelihood of selecting deviant cases, the high-performing districts are no different from the remainder of the districts except for teacher experience. The high performing districts have slightly less experienced teachers, but this difference is minimal and in the wrong direction, so cannot begin to account for the nine-point difference in test scores.

A series of nine SWLS regressions were run with these data, downweighting the average cases by 0.1 and eventually resulting in weights of 1.0 for the high performers and 0.1 for the average districts. The results of this final SWLS regression are found in Table 7.10.

140   Kevin B. Smith, Kenneth J. Meier, Jeff Gill

Table 7.8   Determinants of Student Pass Rates—Linear Model

Explanatory Variable		Coefficient	Std. Error	95% CI
	Outcome Variable = Exam Pass Rates			
	Intercept	55.58657	3.20087	[49.31287: 61.86028]
Environment	Percent Low Income	−0.32944	0.01639	[−0.36157:−0.29731]
	Percent Black	−0.24617	0.01375	[−0.27312:−0.21922]
	Percent Latino	−0.09915	0.01153	[−0.12175:−0.07655]
Financial	Instruction Funds	0.00172	0.00072	[0.00031: 0.00313]
	Teacher Salaries	0.00062	0.00012	[0.00040: 0.00085]
	Percent State Aid	0.02633	0.00814	[0.01037: 0.04229]
Policy	Gifted Classes	0.27644	0.04368	[0.19083: 0.36205]
	Class Size	−0.47697	0.15063	[−0.77220:−0.18174]
Teachers	Noncertified	−0.16242	0.04465	[−0.24994:−0.07489]
	Experience	0.38500	0.10155	[0.18596: 0.58404]
Year Dummies	1992	−10.79596	0.45321	[−11.68426:−9.90767]
	1993	−4.80061	0.47804	[−5.73756:−3.86366]
	1994	−0.88451	0.50441	[−1.87315: 0.10414]
	1995	4.67604	0.53235	[3.63264: 5.71943]
	1996	9.45879	0.64312	[8.19828: 10.71929]

Multiple R^2 = 0.7691
F = 497.5 on 15 and 2240 degrees of freedom
Residual Standard Error = 6.095 on 2240 degrees of freedom

Table 7.9   Comparison of High-Performing Schools to All Schools

Explanatory Variable	All Districts		High Districts		t-statistic
	Mean	Std. Error	Mean	Std. Error	
Pass Rate	54.896099	12.642804	63.465315	12.173996	−9.95143828
Percent Low Income	45.032092	18.266030	44.652703	18.620668	0.28954536
Percent Black	12.845301	14.289981	11.662162	11.307240	1.44642881
Percent Latino	33.296543	29.027341	32.391892	31.266979	0.41303123
Instruction Money (K)	2.4621117	0.364.04	2.475657	0.379683	−0.50798732
Teacher Salaries (K)	27.835807	2.268874	27.821207	2.355032	0.08823874
State Aid Percent	45.542553	20.307917	45.490991	23.107606	0.03198365
Gifted Classes	6.871011	3.002546	6.833333	3.078780	0.17399843
Class Size	15.578457	1.401642	15.501755	1.516728	0.72217396
Certified Teachers	4.110239	3.358696	4.218919	3.262914	−0.47128624
Teacher Experience	11.524818	1.562020	11.063454	1.521829	4.29078117

7 SWAT in Pooled Analysis 141

Table 7.10 Determinants of Student Pass Rates—SWLS

Explanatory Variable		Coefficient	Std. Error	95% CI	
	Intercept	52.70944	3.68925	[45.47852:	59.94037]
Environment	Percent Low Income	−0.30859	0.02007	[−0.34792:	−0.26925]
	Percent black	−0.30538	0.01790	[−0.34047:	−0.27029]
	Percent Latino	−0.13762	0.01419	[−0.16543:	−0.10980]
Financial	Instruction Funds	7.10354	0.08424	[5.45247:	8.75479]
	Teacher Salaries	0.62851	0.13423	[0.36977:	0.89594]
	Percent State Aid	0.04493	0.00949	[0.02633:	0.06354]
Policy	Gifted Classes	0.30783	0.05218	[0.20555:	0.41011]
	Class Size	−0.36355	0.17928	[−0.71495:	−0.01215]
Teachers	Noncertified	−0.10156	0.05105	[−0.20162:	−0.00150]
	Experience	−0.27821	0.11597	[−0.50553:	−0.05090]
Year Dummies	1992	−11.08900	0.51882	[−12.10590:	−10.07211]
	1993	−6.00024	0.55232	[−7.08278:	−4.91769]
	1994	−2.34829	0.57801	[−3.48119:	−1.21538]
	1995	2.73809	0.61515	[1.53240:	3.94379]
	1996	6.18106	0.74655	[4.71783:	7.64430]

Outcome Variable = Exam Pass Rates

Multiple R^2 = 0.7212
F = 386.3 on 15 and 2240 degrees of freedom
Residual Standard Error = 3.021 on 2240 degrees of freedom

Two findings in Table 7.10 are striking. Although most of the variables change relatively modestly as the weighting process occurs, for instruction funds per student and teacher experience the changes are massive. This observation is reinforced by the slope change graph in Figure 7.5. In the OLS regression a $1000 increase in expenditures per student was associated with an increase of 1.7 percentage points in the pass rate, all other things being equal. In the SWLS regression, an equal sized increase in instructional funds is associated with a 7.1 percentage point gain (an increase of 316%). More than any other factor, the difference between these sets of school districts is in what they do with instructional funds.

The other unusual finding is for teacher experience. Experience, measured as the average number of years teaching, is positively associated with student performance in the OLS regression. In SWLS this relationship drops past the point of no relationship so that the relationship for the high-performing districts is negative. A variety of factors could account for this relationship—perhaps the better-performing schools have been more aggressive at releasing poor teachers and thus have a younger but better-quality faculty. Again, targeted case studies are

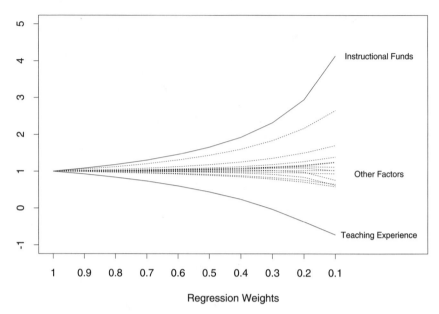

Figure 7.5   Slope Changes—Texas School Districts

needed. The overall impact of this variable on test scores, however, is relatively minor and cannot account for a large difference in the scores.

Our focus on these two variables is somewhat different from what an actual policy analyst would do. The relatively small changes for the other variables can have a large cumulative impact on the performance of a school district. An increase of 70 percent in the slope for state aid is an increase (consistent with other findings for education in this work) that is well worth pursuing.

One other factor of note is the relative increase in the negative slope for Latino students. In the cross-sectional analyses using 1991 data, better districts were able to overcome the differences between Latino and Anglo students. In the pooled dataset, not only did this not occur but the negative slope increased, suggesting that the Anglo/Latino gap was actually wider in the better districts (Latino students on average do better in these districts, with pass rates of 41.7 and 49.9 percent respectively, but the gap between them and Anglo students widens). As noted in the introduction to this section, these districts have experienced a large influx of Latino students since 1991. In all probability, this influx overwhelmed the technologies that were used to get somewhat better results in 1991. For the 36 high-performing districts, as an example, the variable for Latino students is not 95% CI bounded away from zero in 1991, but only becomes so in later years.

7.8 Discussion

This chapter introduced the logic of SWAT to pooled analysis by examining data on two wide but relatively shallow pools. The basic philosophy of SWAT was readily transferable to pooled analysis (Figure 7.6). Pooled analysis gives far more attention to unusual error patterns than cross-sectional analysis (this is a failing of cross-sectional analysis), and seeks to remove as much of this error as possible. SWAT, in contrast, seeks to exploit this heterogeneity.

All the general techniques of SWAT were relatively easy to apply in a pooled context. One key decision is whether to use individual Studentized residuals as the weighting factor or use the mean weights for the entire case. Although individual analysts might come to different conclusions, we found that using the mean weight was preferable. The mean weight made it more likely that the organizations that were selected were consistently high performers. This does not mean that they could not have had very favorable environments (on variables not included in the production functions) for six consecutive years, but the odds of that are unlikely. The use of mean weights, therefore, is generally to be preferred.

7.9 Addendum: Data Description

This section provides the sources of the data, a description of the variables, and a description of how the indices are created. The data and software to replicate the analysis in this chapter are available at http://www.calpoly.edu/~jgill.

Homicide Rate—Homicides per 100,000 of the state population. Source: Federal Bureau of Investigation. Annual. *Uniform Crime Reports for the United States*. Washington, D.C: U.S. GPO.

Population Structure—An index created by factor analyzing state population size and density. Details can be found in Smith (1997). Source: U.S. Bureau of the Census. Annual. *Statistical Abstract of the United States*. Washington, D.C: U.S. GPO.

Resource Deprivation—An index created by factor analyzing state percent black, state percent in poverty, and state per capita income in constant 1984 dollars. Source: U.S. Bureau of the Census. Various years. *Current Population Reports*. Also, *Statistical Abstract of the United States*. Various years. Details can be found in Smith (1997).

Age—Percent of the state population between the ages of 18 and 44. Source: U.S. Bureau of the Census. Various years. *Current Population Reports*. Series P-25. Washington, D.C: U.S. GPO.

Unemployment—Percent of the state population that is unemployed. Source: U.S. Bureau of Labor Statistics. Annual. *Geographical Profile of Employment and Unemployment*. Washington, D.C: U.S. GPO.

144 Kevin B. Smith, Kenneth J. Meier, Jeff Gill

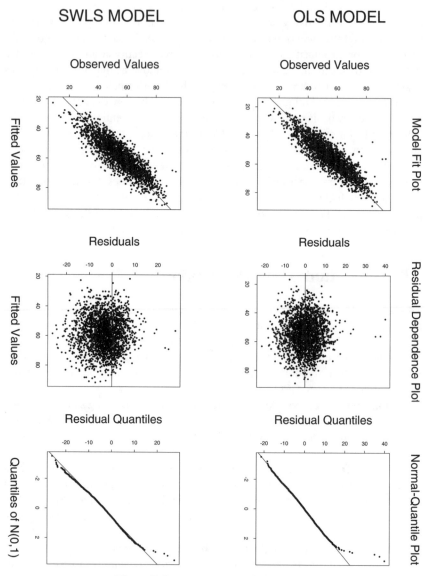

Figure 7.6 Diagnostics for School Models

Divorce—Divorces per 1000 of the state population. Source: U.S. National Center for Health Statistics. Annual. Source: *Vital Statistics of the United States*. Washington, D.C: U.S. GPO.

South—Regional dummy with 1 indicating membership in the Confederacy.

Death Penalty—Dummy variable with 1 indicating a capital punishment state. Annual. Source: *Sourcebook of Criminal Justice Statistics*. Washington, D.C.: U.S.GPO.

Prison—Prisoners sentenced to at least one year per 100,000 state population. Annual. Source: U.S. Department of Justice. *Sourcebook of Criminal Justice Statistics*. Washington, D.C: U.S. GPO.

Income Equalization—Average annual state per-recipient AFDC payment, measured as a percentage of per capita income and lagged 15 years. Annual. Source: U.S. Bureau of Economic Analysis. Various Years. *Survey of Current Business*. Washington, D.C: U.S. GPO, and U.S. Social Security Administration. *Social Security Bulletin*. Washington, D.C.: U.S. GPO.

Education Commitment—Total elementary and secondary revenues from state and local sources as a percentage of total state income, lagged 15 years. Various Years. Source: *Survey of Current Business*, and National Education Association. *Rankings of the States*. Washington, D.C: NEA Research Division.

Executions—Number of executions in a state. Annual. *Sourcebook of Criminal Justice Statistics*. Washington, D.C.: U.S. GPO.

7.10 References

Agnew, Robert. 1995. "Testing Leading Crime Theories: An Alternative Strategy Focusing on Motivational Processes." *Journal of Research in Crime and Delinquency* 32: 363–98.

Baltagi, Badi H. 1995. *Econometric Analysis of Panel Data*. New York: Wiley.

Baltagi, Badi H., and Jame M. Griffin. 1984. "Short and Long Run Effects in Pooled Models." *International Economic Review* 25: 631–45.

Beck, Nathaniel, and Jonathan N. Katz. 1995. "What to Do (and Not to Do) with Time-Series-Cross-Section-Data in Comparative Politics." *American Political Science Review* 89: 634–47.

Blumstein, Alfred. 1998. "U.S. Criminal Justice Conundrum: Rising Prison Populations and Stable Crime Rates." *Crime and Delinquency* 44: 127–35.

Blumstein, Alfred. 1997. "Interaction of Criminological Research and Public Policy." *Journal of Quantitative Criminology* 12: 349–61.

Chaires, Robert H., and B. Grant Stitt. 1994. "Paradigmatic Concerns in Criminal Justice." *Journal of Crime and Justice* 17: 1–22.

Devine, Joel A., Joseph F. Shelley, and M. Dwayne Smith. 1988. "Macroeconomic and Social Control Policy Influence on Crime Rate Changes, 1948–1985." *American Sociological Review* 53: 402–20.

Dielman, Terry E. 1989. "Pooled Cross-sectional and Time-Series Data Analysis. New York: M. Dekker.

DiIulio, John J. 1995. "Arresting Ideas: Tougher Law Enforcement Is Driving Down Urban Crime." *Policy Review* 74: 12–16.

Ehrlich, Isaac. 1975. "The Deterrent Effect of Capital Punishment: A Question of Life and Death." *The American Economic Review* 65: 397–417.

Fording, Richard C. 1997. "The Conditional Effect of Violence as a Political Tactic: Mass Insurgency, Welfare Generosity, and Electoral Context in the American States." *American Journal of Political Science* 41: 1–29.

Greenwood, Peter W. 1998. "Investing in Prisons or Prevention: The State Policy Maker's Dilemma." *Crime and Delinquency* 44: 136–42.

Land, Kenneth C., Patricia L. McCall, and Lawrence E. Cohen. 1990. "Structural Covariates of Homicide Rates: Are There Any Invariances Across Time and Social Space?" *American Journal of Sociology* 95: 923–63.

McCall, Patricia L., Kenneth C. Land, and Lawrence E. Cohen. 1992. "Violent Criminal Behavior: Is There a General and Continuing Influence of the South?" *Social Science Research* 21: 286–310.

Meier, Kenneth J. 1998. "Drugs, Sex, Rock and Roll: A Theory of Morality Politics." Texas A&M University, typescript.

Petersilia, Joan. 1995. "A Crime Control Rationale for Reinvesting in Community Corrections." *Spectrum: The Journal of State Government* 68: 16–27.

Pindyck, Robert S., and Daniel L. Rubinfeld. 1991. *Econometric Models and Economic Forecasts.* Third edition. New York: McGraw-Hill.

Sayrs, Lois. 1989. *Pooled Time Series.* Newbury Park, CA: Sage.

Skolnick, Jerome H. 1995. "What Not to Do About Crime—The American Society of Criminology 1994 Presidential Address." *Criminology* 33: 1–15.

Smith, Kevin B. 1997. "Explaining Variation in State-Level Homicide Rates: Does Crime Policy Pay?" *The Journal of Politics* 59: 350–67.

Stimson, James A. 1985. "Regression in Space and Time: A Statistical Essay." *American Journal of Political Science* 29: 914–927.

Walker, Samuel. 1985. *Sense and Nonsense About Crime: A Policy Guide.* Monterey, CA: Brooks/Cole.

Chapter 8
The Zen and the Practice: Some Final Remarks

Jeff Gill, Kenneth J. Meier

8.1 Overview

SWAT is a new system for analyzing data, but not a completely *original* system; it rests on two familiar pillars. The qualitative pillar is well known to practitioners and basically represents the paradigm that if we are interested in understanding organizational success we should look at those cases that perform well given their resources. This approach is qualitative because it requires identifying the *individual* cases of interest and inspecting their practices. In general, this process works well. However, there are two common instances in which difficulties arise: when the number of cases to sort through is large, and when the definition of success (given the allotted resources) is elusive. These situations lead to a need for the second, quantitative, pillar. We employ a modification of the linear regression model to fill this need. Classical statistical procedures are particularly useful in sorting through large datasets and in classifying specific cases. So an effective combination of the qualitative and quantitative approaches can provide a powerful data-analytic tool.

Our synthesis of these divergent approaches rests on the premise that weighting high-performing (or some other category of interest) cases more than cases of lesser interest, leads to models that highlight the *reasons* that these cases are

148   *Jeff Gill, Kenneth J. Meier*

high-performers. The model therefore does not dismiss average performance, but instead borrows strength from such cases. This idea is vastly superior to that of identifying some high-performing cases and dismissing the rest: having more relevant data is always better.

Although SWAT does not produce estimates of underlying population parameters, we are often not interested in these values. Public managers, policy analysts, and other people who study administrative and organizational performance are often interested in prescriptive results rather than typical results. SWAT allows these practitioners and researchers to determine what is the subgroup of interest, how strict should the selection criteria be, and how reliable and different are the characteristics of that subgroup.

This returns us to the "Zen" of SWAT analysis. There is no implied mysticism here, but rather a philosophical idea that the data reveal different perspectives to different approaches. Contrary to the approach necessarily embedded in most introductory statistics texts, there is no one right way to analyze a dataset (although there are clearly many *wrong* ways to do so). The epitome of the "cookbook" doctrine is the chart on the inside cover of many beginning books that show a matrix indicating the level of measurement of the data with the assigned tool. SWAT runs against such rigid doctrine requiring the analyst to "get messy" with the data—to look at graphical output, to try different thresholds, to consider alternative weighting schemes, and to analyze coefficients from hypothetical populations.

8.2 The Secret Life of Residuals

A datum unto itself cannot be considered an exceptional case in any sense. What might be called exceptional in some contexts could be perfectly typical in others. A data point cannot be classified as an exceptional case unless other data points and a specified model are also provided. Actually, it is even more complicated because, as George Box is purported to have said, "All models are wrong; some are useful." So a data point could be exceptional in some regard with one researcher-specified model but not in another, and we never have *proof* that one model is reasonably accurate and the other misleading. Therefore we cannot classify the potentially exceptional data point with any certainty.

So even when we have a single model, and have fit it to the data, what constitutes an exceptional case? In general, the orthodoxy states that the data are segmented into a systematic and a random component by the model specification process. So the better the systematic component, determined by the model, the smaller the effect of the stochastic or uncertainty component. Since the unit of analysis is the individual data point, the magnitude of the stochastic component is the distance— however that is measured—between the observed outcome and that predicted by the fit *for that single point.* In the linear model and its many generalizations, this is simply a Euclidean distance on the outcome variable measure. These values are called residuals, or disturbances, or errors, or stochastic components. This plethora of synonyms is purposely designed to annoy graduate students.

Outliers are nearly synonymous with large residuals, but this equivalence is a matter of convention rather than definition. The distinction lies in the degree of the effect that the large residual has on the fit. If the large residual does not substantially change the slope of the fitted line (or plane or hyperplane), then we say it has large leverage but low influence. In some cases, this point will change the intercept alone. Conversely, if the large residual exerts some change on the slope of the fitted line, then we say that it has large influence.

The way to measure the influence of a data point is not immediately obvious, because a point with large influence tends to pull the fit towards its position in outcome variable measure. That is, it alters the slope of the line to accommodate its position and therefore reduces the residual. So we cannot simply equate large residuals with large influence. The way to escape this conundrum is to jackknife out (temporarily remove) each individual data point and observe the change in the slope of the fit. This is the central approach of the SWAT procedure: look at points whose jackknifed residual—the difference between the observed data point and the predicted fit of the model for that data point not using that data point in the prediction—is comparatively large. These are cases that are exceptional in terms of their behavior relative to the model and the other data points.

SWAT techniques see these exceptional data points as worthy of investigation. Conversely, resistant techniques minimize the effects of the outliers as a way of describing typical data patterns with less subjection to mathematical inconveniences imposed by these outliers. With both techniques (and they are both useful), we strongly suggest that the analyst use exploratory data analysis to reveal patterns in the data before settling on a final model specification.

8.3 Weighting the Artificial

Weighting is something that all of us do all of the time. We weight the importance of one person's advice over another. We weight the probability of capture when speeding on certain segments of the highway. We weight the relative utility of one menu choice against all of the others. But most important, we weight successful cases around us as having better prescriptive information than others. It is this idea that represents the core of the SWAT approach.

There are an infinite number of ways to develop a weighting scheme, either statistically or qualitatively. We take some inspiration from Jeffreys (1948) and De Finetti (1961), who independently observed that weights should decrease smoothly as the size of the residual in some analysis increases. Jeffreys in particular spoke of reweighting iteratively based on some modifying criteria. The SWAT approach

150   *Jeff Gill, Kenneth J. Meier*

takes this guidance quite literally by cycling through iterated analyses, evaluating weighted implications each time. The generalized substantively reweighted least squares version of SWAT is clearly the most flexible in this regard.

Weighting in SWAT is completely flexible and completely at the discretion of the analyst. At one extreme is the standard linear model with uniform weighting, and at the other extreme is a completely qualitative approach of looking at one case at a time, which represents weighting one case at unity and all the others at zero. The only admonition is that the researcher should fully inform the audience or readers what the selected weighting criterion was.

8.4 Hypotheses

The observant reader will have noticed that we never explicitly test a point-null hypothesis in this work: null hypothesis significance testing (NHST) as practiced in the social sciences is deeply flawed and greatly misunderstood (Bakan 1960; Cohen 1994; Gill 1999; Hunter 1997; Rozeboom 1960; Schmidt 1996). The primary pathology is the mistaken belief that the smaller the p-value is (the probability of the observed data given the null is assumed true), the smaller the probability that null is true. This fallacy is called the inverse probability problem because it amounts to switching the order of the conditional probability statement: $P(D|H_0)$ versus $P(H_0|D)$, where H_0 denotes the null hypothesis and D denotes the observed data. The even more odious manifestation of this misunderstanding is the belief that more "stars" indicate a progressively smaller probability that the null is true and that some coefficient is therefore more likely to be reliable.

We avoid the bulk of the problems associated with NHST by presenting statistical results using confidence intervals. Confidence intervals are an alternative to NHST that provide exactly the same information and more, without requiring a contrived decision. We use the word "contrived" here because making statistical decisions without a specified loss function—i.e., some criterion for the cost of making the *wrong* decision—is not really making a decision. Policy analysts, and others who use data and models to reach some substantive conclusion, live in quite a different world. In our running example, it is clear that the decisions that public school administrators make about resource allocation have clear potential costs and benefits with regard to the education of children.

In addition to confidence intervals, we have argued the strength of empirical findings with various graphical tools: slope change plots, multiregression barplots, residual diagnostics, index plots, casement displays, and density plots. These provide consumers of SWAT analysis with intuitive assessments of what the data are saying through these models. As a data reduction tool, graphical presentations provide the quickest way to communicate findings to readers with a wide range of expertise.

8.5 If I Had a Hammer

We have presented a limited number of different SWAT applications in this book, but have at various points in the text noted other situations where SWAT might also be used. The full range of SWAT uses will be apparent only when the technique is in general use and individual analysts determine whether or not it will be useful to the questions that are analyzed. This section notes a few additional areas and types of problems where we think that SWAT could provide some interesting policy leverage. Any situation where one is concerned with behavior or actitities that are relatively rare appears tailor-made for a SWAT approach. For example, Bohte and Meier (1999) examined a process they called "organizational cheating." It involved school districts that improved their test scores by increasing the number of students who were exempted from taking the test. The overall level of such cheating that they found was relatively rare; most organizations did not take all the legitimate exemptions that they were entitled to take. Cheating, as a result, appeared to be the result of a small number of fairly deviant organizations. A situation such as this, where a small group of organizations appears to be operating in an unusual manner, is a good opportunity to apply the SWAT methodology. Because most organizations are not cheating, relationships between the causes of cheating and the actual behavior are likely to be attenuated. Perhaps such relationships will not even show up until the SWAT weighting emphasizes them.

Although we have not examined individual behavior in this book, we think that any policy that deals with rare behavior on the part of individuals will be informed by SWAT techniques. One illustration is political participation. Objectively, one would think that relatively common forms of participation such as voting would have a different set of determinants than less common and less orthodox forms such as demonstrations and protests. Even more extreme forms of political participation such as violence are also likely to be determined by different factors than the simple act of voting. Again the weighting techniques of SWAT could magnify these behaviors such that important relationships become apparent. The rare-events use can be generalized to what we think of as the rare-events organization. Some organizations deal with highly patterned events—e.g., garbage collection is routine. Other organizations deal only with unusual situations. Disaster management, for example, often deals with unique circumstances as the nature of the disaster interacts with the local environment and the local government's capacity to act. This is quite similar to the distinction in manufacturing between large batch or mass production organizations and small batch or even one-of-a-kind manufacturing. Organizations that deal with rare events will frequently not have enough of these rare events to identify relationships; SWAT may be able to help in this regard. Healthcare policy offers two illustrations of rare events that might benefit from SWAT methods. First, the regulatory review process of the Food and Drug Administration has both effectiveness and safety concerns. In the safety area, situations in which a generally safe drug is toxic might be amenable to rare-event analysis via SWAT. Second, the discipline of epidemiology analyzes the incidence of morbidity and mortality in large populations. The groups affected by an individual disease or other factor that affects individual morbidity or mortality are often relatively small. The huge datasets used in epidemiology often can identify relationships for such factors, but in many cases the profession has to do analysis on less than ideal datasets. When dealing with an extremely rare disease or a limited sample (e.g., individuals with a specified genetic disorder), SWAT procedures could also be useful.

SWAT might also be useful in assessing conditional relationships. For example, Meier and Bohte (2000) were interested in the impact of span of control on organizational performance. They used SWAT to distinguish between effective (better than average) organizations and ineffective (worse than average) organizations. They found that ineffective organizations were more constrained by their organizational structure than were effective organizations. With similar spans of control, an effective organization not only performed better than an ineffective organization, but also was able to tolerate much larger spans of control without ill effects. In short, the relationship between span of control and organizational performance was contingent on the effectiveness of the organization. In this case SWAT was able to reveal the contingent nature of this relationship. Another possible application of SWAT to contingent relationships would be to the study of worker motivation. Herzberg (1968) has argued that those aspects of a job that satisfy a person are different from those that dissatisfy a person. Because these various elements could also interact in a variety of ways, SWAT might be able to sort out the appropriate factors among those highly motivated and those greatly unmotivated. Again, we are very confident that these examples are not the universe of SWAT applications. Policy analysis, we argue in Chapter 1, is an intuitive art. Individuals with experience in different policy areas are likely to come up with SWAT applications that we have yet to imagine.

8.6 The Final Word

We began this work in Chapter 1 with the goal of explaining a new approach to analyzing exceptional cases. Our primary argument there was that the commonly used techniques are in general mean-centered, focused on describing and summarizing typical traits of the data. It is clear that in some data-analytic projects one is not interested in what the average case does, but rather in how exceptional cases came to be exceptional. The public management application is obvious, but there are clearly others.

SWAT is not meant to compete with or replace any other technique, qualitative or quantitative, that readers may be using or considering. Instead, SWAT is a new technique that bridges several traditional approaches. It offers the attractive prospect that some aspect of the data that may be very important to the analyst is now easier to investigate. We hope, therefore, that SWAT sits in the analyst's toolbox among all the other tools.

Our general advice can be summarized as follows:

- Think qualitatively and quantitatively; do not feel compelled to stay in one world or the other when information about your problem lies in both.
- Consider exceptional cases as interesting. There is a *reason* that those points are exceptional.
- Heterogeneity is good; it tells us something about variation and its causes.
- Weighting is a powerful technique for prioritizing the data.
- Look at your data. Look at them a lot. Use as many graphical techniques as you can think of; this is seldom, if ever, a waste of time. In fact, look at them before you specify a model and look at them after you have imposed this model.
- Avoid the deeply flawed practice of null hypothesis significance testing as practiced in the social sciences, including its ugliest manifestations: p-value misinterpretations and "stars" on tables.
- Vary your subgroups of interest. You are likely to be surprised by the behavior of subgroups considered uninteresting prior to the analysis.
- Think prescriptively. The world is full of problems and you have some data.

If there is a final admonition, it would be to read Chapter 1 again. None of the technical discussions or examples will make much sense to the reader unless the message in Chapter 1 is clear. We advise rereading because the philosophy behind SWAT is necessarily new, not because the message is complicated. Complications may arise in individual data-analytical settings as covered in the examples developed here, but they are in general easy to handle.

8.7 References

Bakan, David. 1960. "The Test of Significance in Psychological Research." *Psychological Bulletin* 66: 423–37.

Bohte, John, and Kenneth J. Meier. 1999. "Goal Displacement: Assessing the Motivating for Organizational Cheating." *Public Administration Review* 59 (forthcoming).

Cohen, Jacob. 1994. "The Earth is Round ($p < .05$)." *American Psychologist* 12: 997–1003.

De Finetti, Bruno. 1961. "The Bayesian Approach to the Rejection of Outliers." *Proceedings of the Fourth Symposium on Mathematical Statistics and Probability*, 199–210. Berkeley: University of California Press.

Gill, Jeff. 1999. "The Insignificance of Null Hypothesis Significance Testing." *Political Research Quarterly* 52: 647–74.

Herzberg, Frederick. 1968. "One More Time: How Do You Motivate Employees?" *Harvard Business Review* 46: 36–44.

Hunter, John E. 1997. "Needed: A Ban on the Significance Test." *Psychological Science* January, Special Section 8, 3–7.

Jeffreys, H. 1948. *Theory of Probability*. Oxford: Oxford University Press.

Meier, Kenneth J., and John Bohte. 2000. "Ode to Luther Gulick: Span of Control and Organizational Performance." *Administration and Society* (forthcoming).

Rozeboom, William W. 1960. "The Fallacy of the Null Hypothesis Significance Test." *Psychological Bulletin* 57: 416–28.

Schmidt, Frank L. 1996. "Statistical Significance Testing and Cumulative Knowledge in Psychology: Implications for the Training of Researchers." *Psychological Methods* 1: 115–129.

Index

absolute residuals, 25
Aid to Families with Dependent Children (AFDC), 19
alpha-trimmed, 8, 9, 26
Association for Children for Enforcement of Support (ACES), 19
assumptions, 47

best practices, 34
beta distribution, 45, 46
Bob Wills, 2
boxplot, 52
breakdown bound, 25, 26
bureaucratic capacity, 20

casement display, 125
central limit theorem, 25
chi-squared distribution, 44
child support enforcement, 18
Chow test, 55
conditioning plot, 125
confidence intervals, 20, 150
Cook's distance, 23
cross-sectional dominance, 121

design matrix, 112
design sciences, 2
deterrence, 123
dynamic models, 121

education production function, 85, 103, 104
Edward Jarvis, 50
efficiency, 100
epidemiology, 152
equity, 100, 101, 115
equity measure, 102
errors (disturbances, residuals), 5
Evel Knievel, 7
excellence, 115

excellent agencies, 94
exceptional agencies, 92

F Distribution, 45, 46, 55
failing bureaucracies, 60
failure districts, 67
failure model, 67, 71, 72, 78
Fisher, 50
functional form, 12

gamma distribution, 44
Gauss–Markov, 21, 25, 43
generalized additive models, 3
Generalized Substantively Reweighted Least Squares (GSRLS), 10, 42, 47, 48, 54
George Box, 148

hat matrix, 43
heterogeneity, 6
heteroscedasticity, 76
Huber M-estimator, 26

ideal case, 34
ideal type, 17
identity matrix, 43
incarceration, 123
influence, 23, 149
instability, 19

Jack Nicklaus, 8
jackknifed or externally studentized residuals, 23, 28, 42–44
jackknifed variance, 45
jittering, 105

L_1 regression, 26
L-regression, 35
Land model, 124
learning rates, 19

156 Index

least absolute errors (LAE) estimator, 35
least squares algorithm, 35
least squares with dummy variables (LSDV), 121, 122
leverage, 149
linear programming algorithm, 35
linear regression models, 4, 5
loss function, 150
lucky, 84, 90
lunatics, 50

Markov Chain Monte Carlo, 25
median, 25, 26
median absolute deviation or MAD, 105
median regression estimator, 35
mental health, 50
model fit plot, 65, 129
multiregression barplot, 32, 33, 68, 74, 114

New Public Administration, 100
normal-quantile plot, 65, 128, 129
null hypothesis significance testing (NHST), 150

open system theory, 84
optimizing model, 71, 78
order statistics, 35, 46
ordinary least squares (OLS), 64
organizational cheating, 151
organizational learning, 18, 19, 21
organizational slack, 33, 34
outliers, 25

panel correct standard errors, 121
panel models, 120
parallel relationships, 9
partitioned regression, 8, 9
path dependence, 138
performance optimizers, 66, 72
performance-optimizing bureaucracies, 60
point-null hypothesis, 150
pooled data, 119, 121, 122
pooled estimator, 121
pooled relationship, 130
pooling, 120
population structure, 125
pretty good agencies, 86, 94

quantile regression, 8, 35, 36

R Student, 23
regression diagnostics, 18, 25
rehabilitation, 123
reinventing government, 59
resampling methods, 36
residual dependence plot, 30, 65, 128, 129
residual variation, 11
residuals and influence index plot, 24
resistant, 24, 25, 27, 41, 149
resource deprivation, 125
risk-averse bureaucracies, 60
risk-averse model, 68, 71, 73, 78
robustness, 24, 25, 27, 41
robust regression, 26, 27, 33, 36

Sam Snead, 8
satisficing, 84
scatterplot, 11, 52
scatterplot matrix, 11, 50, 51
scatterplot of the predicted versus actual, 29
sensitivity analysis, 36
skimming, 100
slope change graph, 31, 32, 133
smoothing spline, 50
span of control, 152
Splus/R, 57
spread versus level, 104
statistical significance, 73, 74, 76
Substantively Weighted Analytical Techniques (SWAT), 1, 5, 36, 37, 41, 128
super agencies, 89, 92
Substantively Weighted Least Squares (SWLS), 27–33, 41, 42, 47, 48, 86, 104, 114

TAAS, 139
transformations, 50, 52

weight vector, 112
weighted least squares, 28, 71
weighting, 42, 71, 104

Zen, 2, 120, 121, 148

Index 157